PRAISE FOR BOND OF BROTHERS

Finally, a book for men written by a man. In my humble opinion, *Bond of Brothers* is one of the best books of its kind.

Dave Berg
producer of The Tonight Show

I'm now sixty-eight, and this is a book I needed throughout the decades of my own life. To have it now is a gift of magnitude. This book is rampant with an invitation to trust God and others with yourself, which brings us back to freedom and being fully alive.

Wes Roberts
leadership mentor and CCO of Leadership Design Group

Wes Yoder's book begins anew the conversation about men's twin demons of despair—guilt and shame—and how the power of deeply trusted male friendships can bring hope and restoration.

B. J. Weber
president, New York Fellowship

Manhood and authenticity in our culture are oxymorons. Wes Yoder takes these two and weds them with humor and insight in a celebration of life fully lived without pretense and bravado. If you have a brother, a friend, a father, a son, give him this book as a gift from your heart.

Ruth Graham
author and speaker

Compelling in its elegant honesty, moving in its obvious practicality, and convicting in its unavoidable truth, *Bond of Brothers* drives the reader into the irresistible stream of Jesus' grace.

Cortez A. Cooper
retired minister and Wes's former pastor

Wes Yoder's book reaches out to both men and women. I would recommend this book to anyone who wants to appreciate the love of Christ, his grace, and his mercy.

Kay Coles James
president and founder of The Gloucester Institute

Delightful, transparent trumpet call into the wasteland of battered, individualistic, and broken American manhood. Ring on until the heartstrings vibrate with resonant grace once more. Thanks, Wes.

Richard Showalter
president, Eastern Mennonite Missions

If I had a son, this is the book I would give him. As it is, I'm giving a copy to my dad. I've read plenty of spiritual books for men, but this is the first one that changed my life.

Matt Mikalatos
author of Imaginary Jesus and Night of the Living Dead Christians

Put me down for the first ten sales: one to each of my three brothers, one to each of my three sons, one to each of my four grandsons. And I'll urge their mothers and wives to read it too. Finally, something fresh and real for men.

Jerry B. Jenkins
author and owner of Christian Writers Guild

Bond of Brothers is written by a man who has known betrayal and forgiveness, failure and success. I was intrigued by the powerful stories and applications for my own life. This is a book every man should read!

Darrell Scott
founder, Rachel's Challenge (America's largest school assembly program)

BOND OF BROTHERS

CONNECTING WITH OTHER MEN
BEYOND WORK, WEATHER, AND SPORTS

DON.

WES YODER

May your HEART Live

forever!

ZONDERVAN®

ZONDERVAN.com/
AUTHORTRACKER
follow your favorite authors

ZONDERVAN

Bond of Brothers
Copyright © 2010 by Wes Yoder

This title is also available as a Zondervan ebook. Visit www.zondervan.com/ebooks.

This title is also available in a Zondervan audio edition. Visit www.zondervan.fm.

Requests for information should be addressed to:

Zondervan, *Grand Rapids, Michigan* 49530

Library of Congress Cataloging-in-Publication Data

Yoder, Wes, 1950–
    Bond of brothers : connecting with other men beyond work, weather, and
sports / Wes Yoder.
        p.   cm.
    Includes bibliographical references (p. 187).
    ISBN 978-0-310-32453-9
    1. Christian men—Religious life. 2. Inerpersonal relations—Religious
aspects—Christianity. I. Title.
BV4528.2.Y64   2010
248.8'42—dc22   2010021257

Cover design: Studio Gearbox
Cover photography: Getty Images®, Masterfile®, Shutterstock®
Interior design: Michelle Espinoza

Printed in the United States of America

10 11 12 13 14 15 /DCI/ 22 21 20 19 18 17 16 15 14 13 12 11 10 9 8 7 6 5 4 3 2 1

For my father
For my son
With love to Linda, Jenny, and Mom

Men are shaped by what they love. A man should, therefore, adopt as his first love, as his supreme love, that which he wishes to have shape his heart, his soul, his mind, and his life.

CONTENTS

PREFACE

Welcome to brothers who have been hurt by life, who are stuck and can't quite figure out what to do next.

Welcome to fathers who want to leave an authentic spiritual and human legacy to their children and to the generations they foster.

Welcome to men whose souls run deep but who seldom find the words or the way to say what they really think, feel, and believe to those they care about most.

Welcome to those who wish they could start a conversation with their dads and other men.

Welcome, also, to the women who are willing to listen, to those who want to better understand their men—their fathers, sons, friends, and husbands.

Welcome, especially, to those who have been crushed or betrayed by those you trusted most.

Think of this as your invitation to a new conversation.

INTRODUCTION

GIVE MY DAUGHTER TO ONE OF US? ARE YOU KIDDING?

A MAN GIVING HIS DAUGHTER TO another man "as long as we both shall live" is a scandalous exchange. Pay for the wedding *and* lose the girl? What moron thought up that scenario?

It's all theory until it happens to you, but when it does, the shock evokes a deep silence shared by men around the world. It is a silence that reaches deep into the heart of what a father knows about himself and about other men, and he remembers more clearly at that moment what he was like in his youth than at any other time in his life. The memories can be frightening. Every man who knows himself knows all other men. It's like reading a perfect stranger's mail, whether you want to or not. When that young man asks for *your* daughter, you'd just rather not oblige him.

Maybe it's primal fear, a refined survival instinct. Or that built-in paternal calculator that knows the sum of hundreds of wedding guests does not add up to another semester in Italy. Even so, it's not about the money.

There is something unspeakably beautiful about having a daughter, something as tender as Mother Mary, to whom a rough-and-tumble man is invited. I'll never forget that cool winter morning when the doctor announced Jenny's arrival. "It's a girl," he said. "Are you sure?" I responded. I knew nothing about being a father to a little girl — only that it takes a tenderhearted man to be a good dad for a girl, and I was afraid I might not be gentle enough for what she really needed.

But she grew, and I grew, and somehow, by miraculous design, we waltzed through the years together. I taught her to ride her bike and to forgive a friend who hurt her—so they could remain friends. I helped her with homework and taught her to learn things she thought too difficult for her, talked to her about boys, and all through her junior high and high school years cooked breakfast for her and for her brother. What's a dad to do to spend time with modern kids?

I built her a barn and fenced the pasture for "Sugar," the Christmas horse she got when she was ten. We mucked the stalls together, and when she was seventeen, I held her hand and led that silly horse across the meadow for the last time, crying like a baby, with Jenny comforting *me* of all ridiculous things. "The horse helped me be a better father," I told her. "That's OK, Daddy," she said. "We'll find other things to do together." We hoped Sugar would be the grace that drew another father and daughter closer.

In my religious tradition and in many others, the father is the spiritual leader of the family. It is his honor and privilege to provide shelter and wisdom in the storms of life and to exhibit the love his family needs so that his children will not run to the arms of others to explore love (or some poor substitute) too early. Then, on some bright, sunshiny day, if he has a daughter, it falls on his shoulders to give her graciously into the arms of her beloved in front of God, the relatives, and the entire watching world.

It's not as easy as it looks. Nor is it easy to talk about, especially when no man before you or near you has spoken a word of what it was like for him.

The guy gets the girl. What a happy day—and he won't think another thought about what it cost her father to give her to him until it is his turn, his daughter, and his guts on the line. The most I got from one friend, a writer, on what it was like for him was one word—*frightening*—and an unintelligible grunt from another. I now understand both the word and the grunt. My dad told me later that even though he liked my sister's fiancé, he walked her to the altar (rhymes with *slaughter*) as slowly as he could. So did I.

Given that most men are not really talking to each other about much of anything that matters these days, is it surprising that they are not talking about one of the most significant things a man can ever do? In that one highly symbolic and sacred moment for which there are no words, I placed my daughter's hand into the hand of the man she loves and stood down as her primary spiritual adviser "for better or for worse," thereby establishing my legacy and her welfare and, in many respects, setting the course of her life.

Jenny was radiant, shining like an angel. Early in the evening on a perfect summer day, in the meadow where she played for almost as long as we can remember, we stood together one final moment while the music played. And then I did what a man does when he stands with his daughter before God and the man she loves. I did it smiling, knowing, believing, and hoping: I gave my flesh and my blood to one of us.

Consider it no small thing what one man is asked to do for another. May God help us!

ONE

LET'S TALK ABOUT MANHOOD

Where are your zeal and your might?
The stirring of your inner parts and your compassion
are held back from me.

Isaiah 63:15

MY DAD NEVER WAS A BITTER man. For years, he was a legalist, stern about work and faith, but always with a song on his lips and a twinkle in his eye, a smile working the corners of his face. Unlike other legalists we knew, he fought his fears. Ultimately, he was a lousy legalist. His heart just wasn't into it.

In his early years, Dad viewed good behavior and performance equivalent with godliness, external proof of a credible inward and personal experience of faith. The better the externals, the better the proof you really meant it with God. But as the years wore on, the song of his heart gradually melted external performance in exchange for a deep understanding that God loved him and the rest of us, whether we could perform for God or not. You could hear his clear tenor voice while he milked the cows, while driving up the road, in the shop, and for years, day after day, singing around the dinner table with family and friends. Many times, he took the heat with his own relatives for not being strict enough with his boys. His kindness to me saved my life.

The details are no longer important because it is his story to tell, but it took Dad close to seventy years of his life to learn to walk in complete truth with his family. How long has it taken me? You? All I know is that now my dad is a free man, and his freedom has much to do with mine, as you will see. Your children are connected to you, for better or for worse, in the same way.

Over the years, I've had more than a fleeting thought that I should run from writing this book, but I have resisted the vacuum of silence. I like hiding in my quiet little world as much as you do, and going public with honest thoughts and ideas that are still under construction might destroy any remaining illusion that I have my act together. Instead, I have decided to help create a conversation about what I see as the architecture of a man's heart and soul and to help men find a language that expresses who they are as men in order to restore their families and their dreams, even if, as James Taylor sang, their dreams lie like "flying machines in pieces on the ground."

I know with all my heart that men who have been broken but have not allowed their hearts to become bitter are more useful in the kingdom of God than those who have not yet been broken. They are also invariably more pleasant, and perhaps I can help a bitter man become a better man with a renewed sense of purpose and hope. Perhaps together we can overcome our fears.

Much of what I know I learned the hard way, in "the university of hard knocks, the school that completes our education," as Ralph Parlette put it. My brothers on the journey and I are like men wrestling in a desert night with angels, as Jacob did. Just before dawn, his final rasping cry was "I will not let you go unless you bless me."[*1] He emerged from that unlikely match with a limp, but also with a blessing pronounced on him by God. If you look into my life and yours, you will find that both of us limp as well. Perhaps you have already discovered that God has blessed you and kept you and healed you and has poured his grace into your heart, and that he continues to do so

---

* Source citations for these biblical references are found in the back of the book.

day by day. Perhaps that seems like an impossible dream, good for me or for someone else but too distant to experience yourself.

You, valuable brother, are the reason I have decided to write our hearts and souls into this book about men, about the stuff we don't talk about, in order to capture that which has been stolen from us—our families, our children, our grandchildren, and our friends. This book about the struggle to become a man, to understand ourselves, to be alive in our manhood, is for you, and for all of us.

LIKE FATHER, LIKE SON

The man every guy should know best—his father—is likely the man he knows least. Too often, our fathers walk through our lives as silent heroes or mysterious, distant figures. Male, but undefined; man, but opaque in silence. How often have you heard or said, "My dad doesn't say very much" or, "I didn't know my father all that well"? This is a cry that grows from a wince in the heart of a young boy to something much worse in the chest of a grown man, finding himself falling into the pattern of "like father, like son," wishing he could call that man "friend."

> **The man every guy should know best—his father—is likely the man he knows least.**

When my dad was eighty-nine, he told me that his father, a stern but devout man, complimented him only once. He remembers the moment like it happened yesterday, and the words to him are like fresh-spun honey.

"What did you do to earn such high praise from my grandpa?" I asked.

His face lit up. "I stacked the sheaves of wheat on the wagon better than any of my eight brothers," he said.

While I realize that's a pretty nice compliment for a farm boy from a big family, I said to him, "Dad, try to imagine what it would have meant had Grandpa commended you, say, just ten times during your childhood rather than once. What would that have been like?"

"I don't know."

Such expressive love was beyond his comprehension. Even though he was eighty-nine years old, I could still hear in his voice the longing of the son for life-giving words of grace and truth from his father.

Some time later, I asked him another question. "Dad," I said, "you've told me several times you knew your father loved you. How did you know? Did he ever *tell* you he loved you?"

"No," he said, "I never heard those words." His voice trailed away.

"Not even when you were grown and had a family of your own?"

"No. Not even once." Dad paused. "But I always knew he did. When I was drafted in 1941, he told me he wished he could go in my place."

That my dad eventually discovered an entirely new way to live is remarkable.

Nearly every man I know can recite word for word a beautiful compliment or a harsh criticism received from his father. He can quote it precisely, half a lifetime later. Words, especially those spoken by a father, have the power to break or to heal the human spirit. With words, spiritual strongholds are formed, and by them spiritual legacies are created, good and bad. Words have the power to shape the entire course of a child's life, and fathers hold the keys of life for their children. To withhold from them the simple elegance of a compliment, a hug, or an "I love you," whether they "deserve" it or not, is a sentence of death. It is an emotional and spiritual death, but a death nonetheless.

Fathers hold the keys of life for their children. To withhold from them the simple elegance of a compliment, a hug, or an "I love you," whether they "deserve" it or not, is a sentence of death.

If what we say, who we are, and what we do are the three things by

which we will be remembered, see if this describes you or your father
(or most of the men you know):

- We don't show our hurts.
- We never cry.
- We have a hard time expressing compassion or how we really
  feel.
- We seldom, if ever, give an unqualified compliment.
- We do not feel respected.
- Our language does not include words as simple as "I love you,
  son. I'm very proud of you."
- We talk about our golf games or the weather as if they are the
  most important topics, but the truly significant events of our
  lives as men lie hidden somewhere beneath the surface, invis-
  ible to our sons and daughters, invisible even to ourselves.

We are silent.

THE SILENCE OF MAN

The things men don't talk about are some of the most important
things in life. They are clues both to our sorrows and to traits we
esteem but cannot achieve, to things we love and things we fear. But
rarely do conversations among men drill down to this place where the
good water flows. It may also be true of women, but I have observed
among men and in my own life that the things men do not talk about
eventually become their secrets. Our secrets become our fears, and our
fears in turn become the solitary confinement we exchange for home.

Even more disturbing and damaging than the pandemic physical
disappearance of men from their families is their retreat into mute-
ness, their descent deep into the underworld of insecurities, lost or
dark romance, discouragement, failure, depression, and evaporated
dreams. Over time, as every man knows, the silence within develops
a mind and commanding voice of its own and seeks to become his
master.

The proof of our lives raises no argument against these proverbs: "As he thinks in his heart, so *is* he"; "out of the abundance of the heart the mouth speaks"; and "whoever isolates himself seeks his own desire."[2] Should we assume all our silent brothers have no abundance of the heart, nothing to contribute to a conversation, no words by which to encourage a friend, a son, a daughter, or a wife? Some of us are closed for the simple reason that we have not yet found our voices; we did not know men *have* voices anyone cared to hear.

The things men don't talk about are some of the most important things in life. They are clues both to our sorrows and to traits we esteem but cannot achieve, to things we love and things we fear.

The cause of silence, for others, however, is much more profound. We know that when our hearts are crushed within us, we have no desire to say anything at all. Intentional self-isolation, however, is seldom benign, and it will reveal its hideous fallout given time.

When it really counts, many guys are MIA. We work as long as it takes to provide for our families. We will take a bullet for our wives and children if necessary or work forty years at the most boring job on earth to prove we love them. And love them we do, but years of silence from our dads and from our own hearts leave us with little of substance. Some men throw up their hands and resign. Others just burn down the reservation and everything on it. That we have nothing to say, of course, is the lie we have accepted about ourselves. Just when men reach the place in time when they have the most to offer others, they are ushered to the greatest silence of their lives and think they have nothing to say. Nothing could be further from the truth.

From my conversations with men, I have found that if I know my own heart and am honest about what I find there, I also know what is in your heart, as well as in the heart of every man I meet — and so do you. Not fully, not perfectly, but we know. This is the key to unlocking your own heart, to ending your own silence, and to understanding your brothers, who struggle in the quagmire of their own delusion.

Face it, men will never outtalk women—and we don't need to—but finding his voice is one of the most significant things that can happen for a man, his wife, his children, and his friends. This awakening of soul and mind, rediscovery of dead and lost dreams, rebirth and healing of relationships, and renewed flow of life and joy in a man's daily life are not only possible; they are imperative—and these are not as far from your grasp as you may think.

SAD FACTS ABOUT MEN

Meanwhile, welcome to the emotional and spiritual jailhouse of the twenty-first century. Welcome to the "Utopia" promised to the children of the 1960s revolution, to a world behavioral scientists promised would become extinct. Welcome to one of the most confusing times for men in the history of the world.

For the past several decades, television, pop culture, books, and mass media have made fathers the butt of bathroom jokes and objects of ridicule. Some things about men *are* funny, and some things can be downright bizarre, so there's no need to lose your sense of humor. But as spouses betray their marriage vows, as fathers leave their families, and as men become even more silent about life's essentials, it's time that men rediscover their voices, their hearts, their minds—yes, their souls.

How would you describe the human male? What, if anything, did your dad tell you being a man is all about? What song, what book, what beer commercial, what sermon delineates the real man? What have you or will you tell your son? What have you heard that could not also be said of a woman? Be good, be kind, be godly, be strong, be gentle, and follow your dreams. See the problem? Men aren't talking about or even sure what it takes to be a man, and if *we* don't know, you can bet no one else knows.

A friend told me recently, "It is not exaggerating to say that the condition of men accounts for the world's being in the mess it's in." I've watched men in their careers, guys in high-wire leadership positions in business, politics, media, and entertainment, men who are distinguished in the church and in the community. I grew up with men who were mostly "average working guys" living from one paycheck to the next, and you can bet on the fact that there is a thread running through men, regardless of life status or position, an identifiable common core that has been torn, ignored, abused, or ridiculed. Most of us are hiding—or hiding something—and our default setting if anyone gets close to the real issues is to avoid talking about it. Sound familiar?

Ever since Adam hid from God in the garden of Eden, the natural inclination of every man is to hide, even when we have nothing to hide. So you can bet your life we will hide when we have good reason. It's part of the old world. It appears both in our DNA and as part of our early training. We own it. Once the hiding has begun, the easiest thing in the world is to continue. It soon becomes a deft survival tactic in a brutal world.

Ever since Adam hid from God in the garden of Eden, the natural inclination of every man is to hide.

Despite what you may feel, your value as a man is immense, no matter the turmoil you currently face in your life. If you do not have faith to believe that about yourself for the moment, borrow a bit of faith from a friend and let him help you carry your burden. It is time for you to stop telling yourself the same old lies and begin to believe truth that will set you free. Remember, you are on a journey, not trying to solve a formula, so let's take this one step at a time.

THE ROAD TO BEING A MAN

Reaching manhood is an odyssey. It is a journey requiring courage, honor, and dignity, and it cannot be completed without pain and strife. There is no miracle formula by which a boy becomes a man, or a precise age when he does, but what a guy does with the pain in his life is a major key to finding the doorway to manhood.

Coming to the peculiar state of manhood is like a migration through an unknown wilderness. All along the way there are survival stations and markers from men who've been there before you; it's just that they forgot to leave the navigation equipment you need for the next leg of the trek.

Not until much later could I say with full confidence that my journey in manhood reached some level of maturity that was missing in my younger years. I suppose I will look back on these days when I am twenty years older and say, "Yes, that young man who thought he was old then knew something good about his manhood, but look what he has learned in the two decades that followed."

I'm not sure of the day or the hour in which I became a man. In fact, I know it wasn't on any particular day of my life, and I know for sure it was not on the day I gave my body to a woman. Men who use their sexuality or sexual prowess as the defining mark of their manhood border on relational insanity. The man who says to a woman, "Give me your body; make a man out of me," and the woman who looks to a man to define her femininity by saying, "Come into my body and make a woman of me," are both lost in the swamp. This is the sad depth of our attempt to borrow something we are already becoming but do not understand. Siring a herd does not make a moose a bull. He is a bull because of his native attributes, because of his gender. Unlike the animal kingdom, ours is both a physical *and* spiritual journey, and because it is, I have to neither sire a herd nor shoot a moose to become a man. This dynamic combination of a continuing spiritual and physical journey constitutes the mystery of our manhood and of our existence. Yet even so, while our journey is uncertain, our destination is not. There is good news. A man matters more than the capacity of his physical body to perform his fantasies. He is more than the sum of his failures.

One of my almost-old friends, who will soon be trapped by his inadequacies, told me not long ago, "I want nothing more than to live on a Caribbean island and have lots of sex. I'd like my wife to come live with me," he said, "but if she doesn't, I'm going to have sex with or without her." Good luck, George. I'll check back with you in a few years to see how that's working for you. I'm afraid we're going to have to dig a little deeper to discover who we really are and what really matters.

The great American god of choice actually requires something of you, as does the one authentic God, your Creator, who places your ultimate life choices before you. You have decisions to make about what kind of man you will be. You have options. What you do not get to decide is the nature of the pain you will encounter on your journey. Good choices along the way can lessen the pain, but no man has the power over his own life to avoid the pain that invades the place within him where the spark of a man's soul either bursts into flame or dies.

In the end, if you are a man at all, you will be an honest man. Or you will be dishonest, something less than a complete man, with a dead or dying heart. Not even you can fully convince yourself you are a real man as long as your heart is dead. But the choices are yours. You will be false, or you will be true. You will be hard, brittle, and acerbic, or you will be strong, gentle, and true. You will be authentic and present in the circumstances and relationships of your life, or you will be a counterfeit, irrelevant, and emotionally absent man when it really matters. You will display courage in the face of danger, or you will fold in fear. You will demonstrate dignity and honor, or not.

If you are like other men (and I promise you are), as you continually mature, you will find you are strong and courageous in one setting and a fearful shell of a guy in another. Don't be afraid to think and to ask yourself what part of your manhood is completely formed and what part must yet grow into the person you really are, into the person God says you are. C. S. Lewis, in his brilliant retelling of the Greek myth of Cupid and Psyche, wrote that we cannot face truth "till we have faces." A real man has a real face, and finding your face is essential. It is also *intentional*. Build a fire with your brothers; identify your masks—your false self—and then throw them into the roaring flames. You'll walk away together with a renewed fire in your hearts for the adventure ahead.

Manhood, then, is first of all about being authentic, for God who created masculinity calls men to be honest and alive in the presence of others, including your wife or girlfriend (one at a time, please, and in the right order). It means being alert and honest, available "in spirit and in truth" to your father and mother, your children, your employer, your brothers, as well as to the guy whose interior emptiness drains the life out of the room at work, at church, or at the club.

Manhood is also about initiating a confessional life, acknowledging "when I am weak, then I am strong" provided such a confession is not the PR you put out to make others think you have expunged the weakness or character flaw you enjoy most.[3] It means allowing your weaknesses to become visible. How else will others know your true strength? Just as you, in a broken world, cannot know the greatest joy there is to know without knowing something about the greatest sorrow in the world, so you cannot know and experience your true strength until your weakness is no longer a precious secret within you. You may as well admit your weaknesses and failures, first to yourself, then to God, and then to those who love you most. They already know. God certainly does.

Don't become or continue to be the invisible man, the dad your family wishes they knew, the one who never said "I love you," the brother who was absent while sitting with us. If you are that man already, today is a new day in which the mercy of God is available for the asking. The specific name of this mercy is friendship. If you're one of the many guys who have much to unload and confess due to years, even decades, of hiding, use discretion. Go see an honest pastor or a respected and licensed counselor. Make sure you don't use your wife or children as the local landfill, but do find a healthy way to begin communicating with them.

There are seasons in life, and not every attribute of a man is visible at every given moment. A single man may not have the privilege of providing for a wife and children, for example. But through the course of life, a man will discover that many of the following characteristics have become true of him. Try asking your friends a few questions about what being a man is all about, and watch where the conversation goes.

At some point in life, being a man includes learning to say what you think about the things you do not want to talk about. It means being an initiator among friends and family about the things that really matter. It means being a provider, a defender, and a spiritual leader for your family and for the poor in your community who cannot do these things for themselves. It means you have the lifelong privilege of practicing kindness, of being a servant, of giving away your life in order to gain it, and of providing identity, strength, and character for your family. A man has the honor of being a keeper of wisdom and a sensible lifestyle, of nurturing a true understanding about God as a shelter from the lies of the culture.

While you wouldn't know it by watching most men, you also have the inherent ability to understand the emotional and spiritual needs of your wife, your children, your associates, and friends. You are unique, a one-of-a-kind man who can understand and practice what it means to be a father and husband and lover of your family. You have the opportunity and responsibility to strengthen your family, your circle of friends, the members of the fellowship where you worship, and your neighbors and to do what you can to guard them from physical, emotional, and spiritual danger.

In my mind, I picture men on their knees before a king in humility and dignity. The monarch says to those kneeling before him, "I knight thee," and forever after, these men are knights, made so by the honor conferred by their king, made so by accepting who the king says they are. It is the honor of kings and queens to knight great men because of their accomplishments—in days of old because of their valor in battle and today because of their unusual accomplishments or contribution to the good of the human family.

But not even all knights discover their manhood. Being a man is about far more than turning in a great performance, although if you are a man, you are or once were inclined toward great accomplishments. (I know, a knight in shining armor riding a horse into the fray of battle compared with the modern version of a knighted pop star riding a piano bench at Wembley Stadium seems to have lost just a little something along the way.)

Back then, knighthood began with a ceremony in which a young man was initiated into the brotherhood of knights who practiced holy devotion to their king. They were warriors, and a king could remove knighthood from a man for treason or cowardice. Such disgrace was often accompanied by death.

Now picture this: You are asked to kneel before the King of heaven—the King of kings and the Lord of lords. You bow before the one who created you in his image. You can no longer hide anything—not the lies, not your failures, not your desires, not your pride, nor your self-indulgences or sins, nothing at all. So you present what you have, which is yourself and the meager collection of treasure you have stored in your heart. You can worship your own image no longer because your eyes now behold the glory of the King standing before you. In his hand is the sword of truth, honor, and courage, and his eyes flash with authority. You come to this moment with so little.

What you bring, frankly, is embarrassing. Before this great Master and King, there remains one simple, honest prayer and hope of your heart. In that moment, as you kneel before him, he says in the strongest yet gentlest voice you have ever heard, "Welcome, my son. I hereby confer on you your manhood. It is a gift for which you were created but could not attain. Thanks for bringing me your treasures. I now give you mine. If you accept the exchange, stand up and enter the freedom I have created for you."

THE GOD DARE

Try it. Try bringing him everything. *Everything.* Dare to hold your hands open before the one true and living God and say, "Lord, take from my hands anything not pleasing to you and place into my hands only those things that are pleasing in your sight. Do anything you want to bring my life into harmony with the original design." These are the prayers of genuine manhood. You will not be disappointed, I promise.

You also know it is true, in part, that you confer your son's manhood on him by letting him know, hear, and experience your deep love for him. You must do your part in this story for the sake of your son, or he may not even believe there is a good King. You must teach him and say, "Son, I love you, and I respect you." You must lay aside your desire for him to be perfect, or to perform, or to change his nasty habits, or to cut his dreadlocks before you grant him the peace of knowing your love and your heart for him. You are his father. He is your son. While you can do this in part for your son, he, too, will have his own day to bow before the King should he wish to receive his own identity and complete his manhood. It is God our Father who completes in us what our earthly fathers have begun or left undone, what we could not do for ourselves. And as you know, God makes no mistakes in these matters.

Still, for those without fathers—and there are many among us whose fathers have left the scene, who have already died without saying those beautiful words, or who for whatever reason are incapable of saying "I love you" — the good news is that our Father will receive you and will confer on you today, tomorrow, and the next day what your earthly father may be (or may have been) incapable of doing for you. One of Jesus' last promises before ascending into heaven was this: "I will not leave you as orphans."[4]

Manhood is the process of becoming who God says you are. And as you become true, you will also be set free. My son once told me, "The truth is enough." He's on his way in manhood, and despite the twenty-nine years I have on him, so am I. The truth *is* enough. It still sets men free.

So join me, brothers, not in another failed movement for men but in the pursuit of our healing and joy. Speak up. Stand up. Get out of your game chair. Reject the voice of fatal temptation to just shut up and hide. This can be our resistance, our gentle but holy rebellion against the status quo, against our false selves, against the caricature others have drawn for us.

> **Manhood is the process of becoming who God says you are. And as you become true, you will also be set free.**

We will be rogue thinkers of a new day for men, of a better way for our families and all humanity and a healthier journey to our destiny. We will be realists, knowing that the journey is hard, that changing the world of men one man at a time may seem impossible, but that if it were not good, it would not be for men to do.

TWO

THE WEATHER IS FINE, BUT *I'M* A LITTLE MESSED UP

GIVING AWAY MY DAUGHTER, JENNY, AT her wedding was my wake-up call. If my friends and I were not talking about giving our daughters away, I wondered, what else are men not talking about? The list gets scary.

If you think about it, you can learn more about some men by what they do not say than by their words. A veteran network news producer in New York once told me that she worries about her husband and spends much of her time and energy helping him find friends. He just can't keep the conversations going and isn't close to anyone. The sad truth about lots of guys is we don't have close friends and don't have a clue how to get one. We're ashamed of the stuff we hide and insecure about who we are. We may have a few guys who will carry our coffin when we die, some weekend beer-drinking buds, a few brothers who pat us on the back in church, but no one we actually talk to, no one who will talk to us about anything important.

Conversations among men often begin and end with, "Can you believe this weather?" "How 'bout them Giants?" and "How's that job going?" The perfect conversation for men with little to say can be summed up in eight words: "Can you believe the weather at that game?" If you're a guy, you know, and I know, it's time to start a new conversation, one leading to discovery of our identity, renewal of our hearts, and real friendship instead of more shell games where every player loses because there is no goal, no ball, and no team. I once heard a young man at his father's funeral say the best talks he ever had with his dad were about sports. I wanted to cry his tears for him until he learns to cry.

Game talk provides a kind of recreation or surface friendship for guys who enjoy the thrill of the game and admire a great athletic performance. By some trick of the mind, game talk also introduces competitive behavior within acceptable social boundaries, separating a man from himself and his emptiness for another hour. I'm talking about rules, not exceptions, about excessive sports chatter, not the occasional fun conversation about your favorite team. In some circles, a man is measured by his ability to keep up with this "competition."

For men who measure significance in life by their occupation, a few comments from a guy about his work provide a "read" and enough networking info to continue the chatter, or the signal to move on. These fake conversations, like restless currents in a black water bayou, are not the deep waters of a man's soul. They are social swamps for men. Why millions of men are willing to chat their way through the years in this odd monotone of death, I do not know. But when a man is dead in spirit, there are more interesting conversations in cemeteries in the lonely solitude of the dead.

So what's up with men?

Well, besides the obvious, there is a whole lot of insecurity, secrets, and sadness. And silence. Shame-based silence. This reality cuts across every sector of society, through every religious and ethnic community. We have been consumed with ourselves and with our own gratification while the soulless vampires we create bleed us dry. With the psalmist, we say, "My vitality was drained away as with the fever heat of summer."[1] This is the spiritual consequence of following the path of least resistance.

Take my friend Allen, whose coworker beat up his girlfriend and spent the weekend in the county jail because she "disrespected" him.

"How did she do that?" Allen wanted to know. By going out to dinner with another guy. And what was Allen's coworker doing while he was in his sick relationship with her? Dating three or four other women and sleeping with each of them, which was his "right," he said, yet she was the one disrespecting him by going to dinner with another guy. "His own infidelities," as Stephen King once wrote, "did not excuse hers."

That's bad and common enough among bad characters, but worse is spiritual manipulation of family and friends to hide how sick you are. An acquaintance of mine told his wife the reason he was out late so much was because his friends had all these questions about God. In fact, he said, several had been converted and wanted him to teach them more about the Bible. What was he really doing? His financial records revealed a wide range of late-night sexual liaisons and addiction to pornography. Once a respected man in his community, he now lives on Social Security, alone in his apartment, estranged from his family and every friend he ever had, waiting to die. Every smile is gone from his face, his reason to live dead and gone.

So what's up with men besides secrets involving our fantasies? Why are we so afraid to be known before our weaknesses become a raging nest of hornets? Well, I am sure one book dedicated to starting a conversation among men and those who love them won't cure addictions that need professional help, but let's at least start the conversation. We have almost insatiable appetites for sex, and neither a Victorian nor modern view of sexuality seems to have helped men much. Finding what is healthy and good is essential, but perversion saps our vitality. Our sin is alive and comes looking for us like an old hound dog sniffing us out and barking until someone comes to find out what's wrong. God made it that way, a built-in detector we don't even know is there until it starts howling in the night. Ultimately we can't hide, so why try?

This generation of younger men bears great burdens as they watch their fathers, their isolated and friendless fathers, betray their ideals and character as the images they created for themselves crumble. But what's more, there is a growing anger among young men who are awakening to their losses and are now old enough to understand, because of how they love their own children, the profound loss sired by the silence and disinterest of their fathers. Bewilderment in younger men gives way to anger as their life experience progresses. The supreme disappointment of men who realize they are more mature in relational life skills than their parents brings with it the shocking realization they are now in the role of not only leading their children but also, in this respect, parenting their parents.

The profound strength of secrets to create silence in men is connected to this disturbing trend, and I predict, without some kind of awakening to the devastation we are now experiencing as "normal family relationships," this alienation between fathers and sons, between men and women, and man-to-man will become chronic and produce a more separated society. Hatred has the power to transform us into the very thing we hate.

Sociologists now query the relational effects between technologies and behavior that drive us deeper into isolation. But combine the power of tech-sex addictions with one-third of our men who are not talking about their participation in the destruction of the fetus that they know in their hearts would have been their firstborn son or daughter, and you will encounter one of the darkest and least understood societal game changers of our day. Perhaps in twenty years, when we observe a worsening relational dynamic among men, we will understand this new wrinkle in time, but right now, no one seems willing to consider the consequences. The effects of shame apart from the healing of the soul never disappear from the life of a man but provide the matrix of continuing destruction within him. Our healing is no longer optional if we are to have anything left of ourselves and those we love. Shame-based secrets mar not only our self-image but also our identity. They are the greatest unknown factor in the minds of friends, who think, "I like Jack, but there's something not quite right about him, and I can't put my finger on it." You just have.

When a man has something to hide, the first thing he tries to control is money. Fear is like that. So here's my advice: if you control the money in your family, make sure your wife knows where it is and where you spend it. If you are serious about wanting God to bless you, be generous with your wife and do your best to bless her. Be open about the credit card bills and the bank statements. No secrets. Keep the relationship open, the money trail visible and clean, because most sin eventually costs money—and addictions create poverty.

But this is not another book about sexual fantasies, addiction, or pathologies that turn men into monsters. It is not even that kind of conversation. Instead it is a declaration of war on shallowness and what makes the average guy, well, more average than he should be. It is about finding and renewing your heart, about discovering a language to say what you think and care about. "Keep your heart with all vigilance," Solomon wrote in the book of Proverbs, "for from it flow the springs of life."[2]

But how?

IT'S TIME WE STOP PRETENDING WE DON'T KNOW EACH OTHER

We have the power to make choices that can destroy us, and so we need a new global understanding among men, a new baseline acknowledging that every man who knows himself knows all other men. Because we do, our common confession is that we are messed up—sometimes more than a little. Each man creates his own formula for adding grief to his life, but the ingredients are the same, and the outcomes are predictable. Therefore we acknowledge our need for God and for each other, and we refuse to separate our need for God from our need for our brothers. We confess our faults to each other instead of pretending we have none, and we thereby receive both forgiveness and healing.

This life-giving art of friendship and conversation among men has nearly vanished. Men are dying at parties, wasting time in dead churches, consumed with busy routines, and driven insane with small talk. In the space vacated by healthy friendship and conversation has come the fast pace of the new West, remote controls, and instant global access to the inventive and addictive genius of amusement and entertainment. We can sail through a day, a week, a month, even years, without reading, without a moment for quiet reflection, without having an original thought, without a single authentic conversation.

Every man who knows himself knows all other men.

Blame it on whatever you like—your father who never talked with you, goofy churches with goofy rules not even God would obey and which can do absolutely nothing to make a man spiritual or human, or the cold architecture of greedy contractors who stopped building porches on homes fifty years ago and did their part to destroy conversations with neighbors. Or take responsibility for your own shallowness. Becoming efficient and utilitarian has destroyed our beauty. Mega-everything just isn't fun anymore. Churches have missed the point about men because our life together isn't really about celebration and friendship but about making us look good. Our parties are no better. The women talk about the hot guys in the movies, while the men talk about the babes. We'll yak about politics, sex, and religion and what the bad guys are doing, and "Oh, by the way, what are the kids doing now? How's your swing coming along? You should see my new set of clubs.... Boy, this was a great night." Just shoot me and put me out of your misery. The world is falling apart because of bad parties and bad churches—an overstatement, but barely so. Of course, our issues go much deeper than that, but a few men interested in friendship with brothers who have something worth celebrating can change them both.

The idea that we have nothing to say is not true, but those who have lost themselves along the way tend to be awkward and loud, content with skin and other surface materials, smooth as Teflon or inappropriately silent. Whether we know how to say anything to another man or do not understand or care enough about others to create meaningful channels of communication is another issue. It doesn't take much to make a conversation lively, even with someone you've met for the first time, yet, for guys, friendly conversation can be one of the most awkward experiences of life. Conversation among men that flows easily between the mundane and the meaningful, from weather to religion, from philosophy to art, from game to work, from humor to love, from sadness to anger, and from politics to significance—literally from the sacred to the insane—that kind of conversation is an art, one that diminished with our disappearing porches and is misplaced now in the oblivion of text messaging and twittering. Our "brave new world" where "optimism has driven people into pessimism," as G. K. Chesterton observed, keeps us too preoccupied to develop the thoughtfulness of a broad spectrum of life.

YOUR FACE TELLS YOUR STORY

Whatever the reason, men are insecure about who they are and what they are meant to be. To live is to discover your identity so you can live fully in the presence of others. Why, then, should we rely on our professions, our education or lack of it, our social lives, our churches, or the voices around us to define us? Some voices we hear are honest and astute, yet even kind voices can peg us with a lifelong identity that is not our true self. An assigned identity, except for the one given to you by your Creator, is false. If it is false, it is not true. And if it is not true, it is a lie.

If you've made an agreement with a lie about who you are or if you live within a false self, how then could you have an honest conversation? This is a clue to the reason men do so well talking about weather, the game, and the job and have so little to say about anything else. One friend told me recently she does not think it is possible to have an honest conversation with at least 80 percent of the men she knows. Could be, but discovery of our true person and the potential of our unique manhood is one of the finest adventures in a man's life. It's sort of like hide-and-seek, but a man has to be alive to celebrate the chase. He has to be willing to see himself as he is. When I offer my fake ID to you, I am asking you not only to believe a lie but to believe that my glossy, two-dimensional image is a real man. It's not. We're like children, drawing stick figures with crayons, who say, "This is me, and this is you, and this is the cat" — except children know the difference between stick figures and real people.

When I was a kid, my mother sometimes referred to me as her "little businessman." Fearlessly I knocked on neighbors' doors to sell Mom's homemade bread and the vegetables we grew in our gardens. I enjoyed her compliments and believed in the product. Because I developed a knack for selling early in life, it was easy to take "businessman" as part of my identity whenever I thought about who I was. It only took a few years of married life to realize that my wife and my friends, while interested in some of the successes of my career, really did not want to hear much about what a good day I had at the office last Thursday. I was one of the lucky men who became aware that my performance at work and my career were not my identity. In fact, they have almost nothing to do with who I am, the construct of my soul, or the rock that provides the foundation of my life. The source of my identity is a deeper reservoir, and so is yours.

Over the years, Mom refined a direct yet backhanded way of giving a compliment — backhanded in the sense that you had to stop and think about what she said, and by the time you turned it over in your mind, it was stuck there to serve you for the rest of your life. I was in my early forties when, one day, she looked straight into my eyes — her eyes searching mine, her hands holding my face just a few inches from hers — and said, "Wes, I'm so glad God has delivered you from the little deceits in your life." Layers of wisdom, grace, gentle rebuke, encouragement, insight, hope, love, and motherly affection were wrapped up in that little package. She perceived my life all along, yet she waited and prayed, prayed and waited for years to drop that life-giving bomb. Of course, being "delivered" is an ongoing process for me.

What does a man who understands his identity look like? Who is this man? He is someone to whom you are drawn, yet not so much because of his carriage as his confidence, not so much because of his titles as his kindness, or because of his accomplishments so much as what he has learned from his mistakes. Men who understand their made-by-God identity seem quite average until you look into their eyes or get close enough to see the wrinkles in their faces. Each wrinkle contains memory, the DNA of your soul, traces of salty tears if you are honest, the warmth of years of smiles and laughter if you take pleasure in kindness and understanding, and the marks of wisdom and graces that will carry you safely home. This is the man you are becoming, if you are becoming a man at all. Your face tells your story. Your eyes reveal your heart.

The good news, if you are one of the many guys who do not like what they see written on their faces or in their hearts, is that the end of your story is not yet written. Not quite. You can spend whatever time you have left writing a new conclusion, changing what your face now predicts will be the end, adding sparkle where once there was mostly deadness in your eyes. Face changes follow heart changes, but all fakes get busted. Guaranteed.

So my mom is right. Deceits, especially those I think no one notices, actually prevent me from being the person — the man — I am. It's the odd condition of being who I am but not yet being fully me. At minimum, the guy who wants to be a man, a man who understands his identity, desires a clean heart in which deceit is decreasing and delight, pleasure, and happiness are increasing. He's not perfect, but his feet are pointed in the right direction. The guy who isn't interested in this prescription for a meaningful life can measure himself against the proverb: "Deceit is in the heart of those who devise evil, but those who plan peace have joy."[3] Devising evil or planning peace? Deceit or joy? You decide.

By the time what I call "the tough years" arrive, those unexpected days of struggle in midlife you thought were meant only for other guys, most men expect to have life by the tail. Whatever pain we inflicted on ourselves in our youth is behind us. Older guys between the ages of forty-five and sixty pretty much had things figured out. Excluding a few old nuts who got what they deserved, we imagined them and ourselves at their age to be immune to our own stupidity, enjoying our dreams, safe in a beautiful world of promise. Our fathers did little to divest us of our illusion in which success, the American dream, family, and all the right stuff were together in one place. I saw a poor guy here and there freak out and lose it all because of an ignorant midlife crisis, but I promised myself I would never have one. Every theorem is tested. So is every man.

Every theorem is tested. So is every man.

The fears that come to a man in this season of his life are immense. Will I accomplish my dreams? And what exactly were they again? Does the financial scale have to be so difficult, and why are *my* kids the ones flipping out? What happened to my body, because it's not cooperating like it used to. I'm working harder now than ever, but neither Momma nor the kids seem to notice or care. Why should I? Charles Spurgeon reflected that pain, suffering, and grief may be used in our lives to keep us from sinning. But the truth of this depends on the man and on his heart.

SOMETHING IS WRONG IN PARADISE

Two mind-numbing events welcomed us to the twenty-first century. On 9/11, the terrorists got us, and on October 2, 2006, in Nickel Mines, Pennsylvania, the shooting of ten innocent Amish schoolgirls reminded us how much we terrorize ourselves. Both provided adequate evidence of a world gone mad and introduced our new national midlife crisis, a crisis of both our identity and of our aging ideals. The tragedy of 9/11 and the financial meltdown a few years later made fear a national currency.

Our thoughts the day the towers fell exposed us. The world heard us ask and answer questions that revealed our identity. We wanted to know who hurt us, so that we could hurt them in return. National TV hosts questioned whether we should forgive. Can one nation forgive another? Can a nation forgive a terrorist, or is brute force the only possible response? Are we obligated to forgive if we are not asked to forgive? Our answers made it clear that we prefer to forgive only nice people who do not actually intend to hurt us. Forgiving our enemies is another matter altogether. Forgiving enemies is history splitting, nation splitting, and it seldom happens.

Members of Congress, reflecting the majority view of the people, voted to support a path to war and retribution. Our enemies, we declared, would be brought to justice. This is not an argument for or against the decisions defining our recent history, but it can hardly be said that our enemies who languished at Guantanamo received justice or, on the other hand, any motivation toward becoming our friends. How does one tame a terrorist? More than one national TV program guest said that unless we are asked to forgive, we have no obligation to do so, and many Christians were confused by this. On the one hand, we embrace the right of sovereign nations to make war; on the other hand, we support the notion that peacemakers are declared by Jesus to be blessed. Like it or not, these were our choices, this was our test at the beginning of a new century, a new millennium, the dawn we hoped would bring a more utopian future. War, we soon discovered again, splits a nation more than forgiving our enemies ever has.

Within a few days of the shooting at West Nickel Mines Amish School in the fall of 2006, the Lancaster newspaper ran a feature story on forgiveness, the quaint Christian teaching practiced by the Amish. National media alerted the world that the Amish had sent a delegation to Maria Roberts, the shooter's wife, on the day of the murders to say they forgave her husband and held no grudge against her. Everyone was astonished. How could they do such a thing? Because of their kindness, many doubted the Amish perceived what had actually happened to them, a dismissive and cynical attitude that melted away as the truth became known. It was the day the Amish tutored an entire nation. What they were doing was following the example of Jesus, who, while he was still suffering, prayed, "Father, forgive them, for they know not what they do."[4] The local news story compared the Christian concept of forgiveness with the teachings of other major world religions and included comments from members of those groups. A Muslim said, "We do not really ask others to forgive us, but if we ask Allah, he will forgive our sins." Someone presented the classic rabbinical position on forgiveness, saying Jews do not believe in forgiving others unless they are asked to forgive by the person who hurt them. "Besides, what's the point? Only God can forgive sins," he said. "When people die young," a Hindu said, "there must be a large amount of bad karma to shed quickly. We believe that Roberts and the Amish girls had an affiliation in a past life that needed to be resolved." Instead of being horrified by the shooting, "we should be glad [the bad karma] has been resolved," he said.

In the Hebrew Scriptures, there is a long history of seeking forgiveness from God for one's sins, on making sacrifices on the Day of Atonement, but not an emphasis on forgiving one's *enemy*. The psalms do not mention the concept even once. Instead, the first focus in the Scriptures is on the requirements for justice — an eye for an eye, limb for limb, life for life — and on personal forgiveness from God for one's own sins, which are many. Cities of refuge provided protection and mercy for the guilty. The young Jewish rabbi from Nazareth, however, set the world aflame with the new teaching that those forgiven by God must extend to others the mercy and comfort they have received. Not only that, Jesus made central to all Christian teaching a devastating new doctrine that I may only expect forgiveness of my offenses to the extent I am willing to forgive others their transgressions against me. It is a miserable catch-22. This does not alter his gift to me of complete forgiveness of my sins for salvation, but it does mean I will be bound in resentments rather than full of joy and the freedom that comes when I take my hands off the neck of the guy I won't forgive. God has a way of putting the dunce in the corner and making sure the incarnation never becomes a rusty theological theory. Without forgiving as I have been forgiven, God has tricked me again, allowing my own desires to deceive me and putting me in a box from which I cannot escape.

Jesus made central to all Christian teaching a devastating new doctrine that I may only expect forgiveness of my offenses to the extent I am willing to forgive others their transgressions against me. It is a miserable catch-22.

The man who does not forgive has another problem. He has few friends, and most of them are like him. Forgiving those who hurt and betray you may not mean you become friends with them, yet it may, because a man who forgives is the kind of man who attracts friends. More than a few men will curse the very idea of forgiving an enemy. A man at our church told me he scoffed when he heard me say he had to forgive the guy who stole his wife. It took him a long time to do it, but Craig has become—and is becoming—an entirely new kind of man, and he has genuine compassion for the troubles that have now overtaken his thief.

Forgiveness is complex, and it can be very messy, but as the Thad Cockrell song says, "Pride won't get us where we're going." The reality for those trapped on the hamster wheel of offenses that spins around in their minds, the offense coming back again and again, is that nothing good happens until somebody forgives someone, to rephrase an old line. Forgiveness stops the hamster wheel, gets us off its dizzying ride, and gives us strength to love the scoundrels who hurt us. Love permits us to consider that, while they may still be scoundrels because of their insecurities and misplaced passion, they were lesser men than they were created to be. I must come to believe that unless I can forgive my enemy, I become like him. Unless I can forgive him, I, too, am less than the man I was meant to be. Forgiveness grants passage to both the forgiver and those in need of forgiveness whose engines have stalled on the rails of shame and guilt. Of course, there are times when the perpetrators are real rascals, as close to the devil in the flesh as they intend to be, and that is when the teaching of Jesus takes on a whole new meaning.

Refusal to forgive you for what I lost when you took advantage of me means I do not believe God has anything else to give me. No more friends if this one bails. No more money if you wreck our deal. No more creative ideas if this one is stolen. No more kindness, nothing. I've got to look after myself. If I lose this to you, God cannot replace what was lost. In fact, we're so messed up we actually think it is *God's fault* when others hurt us. Forgiving, on the other hand, is staking my claim in the goodness of God. There's more where that came from, whether money, creative ideas, or relationships.

You can try to forgive and remain in your bitterness — but that does not work. You can try to hold on to your hurt — but that is only self-destructive and torturous. You can try to forgive and still make the other guy pay — but that is cruelty. Or you can forgive in self-righteousness to become one of the violent men who take the kingdom of God by force, as Jesus said, and contaminate others with their sick version of religious rules and guilt to convict and control others — but that is the equivalent of spiritual rape and murder.[5] The only other option is something far more radical.

We are a guilty tribe, yet once we are forgiven, he only requires us to love our enemies and to welcome fellow sinners. To seek more is insane. To pursue less is self-righteous. Yet to guard against such obscene pressures required by Jesus, we hide ourselves in religious rags, but we are still naked. Our nudity obliges us to appoint ourselves as

God's agents to convict and control others, deceiving ourselves and transforming communities of faith into conclaves of religious idiots. But being guilt free in this economy does not mean much to guilt slingers and builders of big programs. They are too worried to forgive, too insecure not to make dependency a primary trading currency, too power hungry to smile, too anxious to live in the shelter of divine mercy. The good news is that in Jesus you don't have to pay for your own sins.

Inscribe *that* thought deep into your soul.

LIFE WORTH CELEBRATING

God, because he is clever and kind, does not require messed-up people to live in a perfect world. His equation instead is this: imperfect people in an imperfect world. The original equation in Eden was perfect people in a perfect world, but on the first day of human imperfection, God subjected all creation to futility. In a moment, his command at Eden created a way for us to survive our brokenness and despair, heartache and toil, anguish and sorrow. There is one example in history of the perfect coming to an imperfect world. The results were predictable—imperfection seeks the death of perfection.

That's where we get messed up. We know there must be something better—our longing proves it—but we don't know how to achieve it. God is a little slow giving us what we want, so we try to take it. That's the effect when two "perfect" people strive for a "perfect" life in an imperfect world: someone is going to die. It's a perfect formula for emotional, spiritual, even physical suicide. If I have just described what you are doing with your marriage, your kids, or even your dating relationship, I recommend you quit it. We *are* messed up, but two imperfect people in an imperfect marriage can have an amazing life together when they quit their silly sham. My marriage is a good example. The same goes for the church, and when those lights finally come on, church and parties and marriages are so much better, so much happier. So are the kids.

Friendship — spiritual friendship — is the life-giving core of all healthy relationships among men. Otherwise we get stuck inside a matrix where our mission becomes more important than the people who are on the mission with us. If friendship is not at the heart of our relationships in our church and religious environment, we become self-righteous and out of touch, like the older brother in Rembrandt's *The Return of the Prodigal Son* who stands above the repentant scene as the isolated and arrogant instructor instead of a penitent member of a messed-up family. Jesus never elevated himself except when he was lifted up on a cross. When people come to us with their problems, we think we have to be smart or spiritual, but what they really need is for us to be present with them in their troubles. God can solve their problems, and perhaps we can help, but being present to comfort, to love, to listen, to take a step toward Jesus together in our brokenness — that is the essence of friendship.

Friendship — spiritual friendship — is the life-giving core of all healthy relationships among men.

Many people will do almost anything to avoid the openness of spiritual friendship. Religion offers the perfect fix for your troubles, but as your friend, I must offer you my weakness. Instead of perfection, I can promise you only brokenness. Together we invite Jesus into our shared brokenness and he — the incarnate Christ of God alive within us — can do the work of remaking what is left of the mess we have made of ourselves.

Most of us are fine with God being so clever and kind, just the sort of god we'd like to hang with for a while. But he does require one thing if we are to enjoy him and to find peace. *He requires us to live.* Even that is our choice. It begins with sitting at his table, entering into his existence, being fed with his bread and his wine. When we receive him in this way, we begin to realize other sinners he has invited to sit with him have also begun to smile, and we know why. When God forgives us, he invites us into his presence. When we forgive others, we invite them into ours. This is how a man moves from isolation to the bond of brothers and to a tableful of friends; and the renewal of the male spirit depends on it. The mess doesn't matter so much when Jesus is with us, and the weather can take care of itself.

THREE

GAME AND STORY—
ENTERING THE
KINGDOM OF GOD

AMERICANS LOVE THEIR GAMES. WE'RE A nation that works so we can play. We buy over $26 billion worth of sports entertainment each year, and trends show we would not mind spending a bit more.* We took a ball, figured out forty variations on a theme, and sassed it up so much that people pay hundreds, sometimes thousands, of dollars to watch one team torment another. These inventive, grown-up versions of "keep away" down at the stadium are amazing, really, if you think about it. Never have men done so much with so little.

I, too, have my favorite teams—the Tennessee Titans and the Philadelphia Phillies—with no explanation for the odd pair except geography and the early brainwashing of Mennonite cousins allowed to listen to their radios at our house on Sunday afternoons when baseball was king. I liked the Phillies because my cousins liked them and because they were on the radio. I am a fan now because I am fascinated by the mysterious dynamic that requires equal amounts of love and hate needed to remain loyal—and by the malevolent force that destroys their winning streaks whenever I happen to check the standings. Because I live in the South, whenever the Phillies beat

---

* Statistics compiled by *Street & Smith's Sports Business Journal* (*www.sportsbusinessjournal. com*). Figure includes cost of tickets, concessions, and souvenirs. Total annual sports spending has exceeded $194 billion.

the Atlanta Braves and make it to the playoffs and beyond, a sinister thread of joy connects me to my Yankee home and to a few hundred thousand other lost guys. I am sure we all need therapy. Offer me tickets to World Cup games anywhere on the planet, and my son and I will be there, cheering like mad fools.

By way of strategy and elegance, baseball is the most sophisticated game achieved by men. It is a highly intense, lazy game. Give me some warm afternoon sunshine, a Ball Park frank, and a drink, and I'll stick with you for the first three innings. I'll be off snoring in dreamland for the next three and will wake up for the end of the game, having missed absolutely nothing.

I'm really not much of a sports guy by modern standards. Sort of a misfit, really. We didn't have Little League, community sports teams, or an organized high school sports program, which had something to do with cows and chores and Momma's good cooking, all higher priorities in Amish Paradise. An elementary teacher once told me I ran too long in the same place and somehow wasn't coordinated enough to compete. I learned to walk jumping corn rows and dodging cow pies in the meadow, not exactly the best preparation for organized sporting events.

Even with these severe disadvantages in my early life, we were at no loss for games of every sort. There were elaborate forts in the haymow, bag tag, riding cows in the meadow, Monopoly, Scrabble, mush ball, hatchet-throwing contests, rotten-egg battles, swimming in Nickel Mine Creek, the mud run behind the house, racing goats pulling little red wagons downhill at full speed, hunting with shepherd-boy slings and a few smooth stones, and plenty of other made-up country games. We played our hearts out as young boys should, so with regard to games, my childhood lacked nothing.

I hesitate to say I ever grew up, but sometime after others thought I had, I became friends with a true-blue sports guy. Ed was our next-door neighbor. To this day, I have not met anyone quite like him. He can quote statistics from multiple sports, remember and pronounce names of actual players and the positions they play, show up at any playoff game in the world with or without tickets and get one of the best seats in the stadium, recite the play-by-play of the Vanderbilt-Texas Tech Peach Bowl game of 1974, and talk about sports all night long. All day and all night, for that matter. For the longest time, I didn't know he could talk about anything else or that he had a regular job, until I discovered one day that he was my banker. His kids were geniuses on the field and could do amazing things like get home runs on infield hits and jump ten feet in the air to catch a football. The glory days for my son in Little League culminated when he threw up on home plate on the first and last run he ever scored. His successful high school football career, both of us know, had absolutely nothing to do with abilities he inherited from my side of the family.

So to have Ed as one of my best friends almost thirty years later is close to a miracle. (It could even *be* a miracle.) Our friendship was unlikely, and one day, about ten years into it, Ed told me I was "the first nonsports friend he ever had." I countered that he was "the first sports friend I ever had." We howled and often laugh today at the crazy combination. I still have no idea what to say to him when he dives into one of his euphoric sports dazes, but I've learned he does not need me to reciprocate by quoting statistics or game trivia to him. He already knows it all, and I can enjoy what he enjoys just by listening. A near-death experience a few years ago turned Ed into a voracious reader. My only fear is a similar experience would turn me into a sports nut!

I am sure, and so is Ed, that our friendship is evidence of the idea that all of life is holy. We were meant to complement each other, each contributing to our friendship something missing in the other. Our friendship represents in a small but accurate way that God's interests for men are healthier than the sports craze endemic to our culture, or the idea that every moment has to include serious spiritual contemplation to be pleasing to God. If all of life is sacred, God may want to do something with men and their games, and happily, I don't think he wants to take them away. But in addition to sports chatter, might he also be interested in hearing a more balanced exchange of ideas and enrichment among men? Our craze over games, a clue that something is missing in our lives together, as much as anything may be the result of a placid spirituality with almost zero appeal to men. Neither provides for men a balance of game and story.

When the main conquest in a man's life is living vicariously through the contest of other men, he has become the victim of a great deceit. Living for the next game, which many men do, won't give us life. A beautiful proverb says, "He who is noble plans noble things, and on noble things he stands."[1] But with respect to sports, we participate merely as spectators, "amusing ourselves to death," as author and cultural critic Neil Postman observed, and stand not in the nobility of the human spirit but in something much less. The rugged spirit of man seen clearly in our games is missing from much of our own lives. Year after year, we pay more than the gross national product of many Third-World nations to watch. We have become a new class of citizens — the great "American watchers" — and as such, we are not "in the game" at all. Left to amuse ourselves with the games of others for more than a full generation, could perhaps the global economic disaster of the early twenty-first century indicate a regressing maturity of our humanity, a misplaced value system, and a slow decay of Cowper's "better hour," whose classic sonnet was penned in celebration of William Wilberforce's lifelong efforts to secure the abolition of slavery in the British Empire? Such decay turns even our entertainment to boredom.

When the main conquest in a man's life is living vicariously through the contest of other men, he has become the victim of a great deceit.

Amusements that possess an entire society point to deeper problems and likely predict more significant outcomes than we yet understand. Obsessions are prophetic. Ignoring the needs of the poor, for example, is one of the greatest casualties of a Game Boy approach to life. Could an entire global society, as *London Times* columnist Matthew Parris writes of Africa without the Christian faith, be left "at the mercy of a malign fusion of Nike, the witch doctor, the mobile phone and the machete"?* Is what we hired to soothe us already a source of reflexive violence? Our sociologists and prophets have more to tell us about this, as do the obituaries of so many of our young sports heroes.

Former Boston College educational psychologist William Kilpatrick calls sports "the emotional center" of modern men. Author Paul Young says a man's natural inclination is to focus on his work and his performance rather than on relationships. Man is connected to the dust and dirt of the earth from which God created him — his "nearest relative source," as Young describes it, the instinctive focus of his post-Eden life experience. This life experience is rooted in struggle and performance. Put the two thoughts together, and you may have a plausible explanation for why men are so attracted to sports performance.

So this mess we have made, this odd place we have created where men are not men, where the primary story we tell is the story about our game, is at the root of much that troubles men in Western societies. It is worth considering to what degree identity with our team, our club, or our corporation has contributed to the lost voice of men, our misplaced identity, and our ruined mission. Do you have a voice others want to hear? Do you understand your own identity or know, in clear terms, the design of your life? The loss of these marks of manhood creates aloneness, souls within men unavailable to us and to others.

Among the lonely sounds I hear from men are the echoes of our own voices cheering temporary "heroes" who pursue our dreams for us. Temporary, that is, because they will betray us in the next round of negotiations for a few more buckets of hot cash. And why should they

* Matthew Parris, "As an atheist, I truly believe Africa needs God," *Times Online*, December 27, 2008.

not? We curse the teams that lose, and half of them lose every week. Then, when individual players are too weak to win, we discard them with barely another thought. These are men, our brothers, and after the game they are perhaps the most broken of all men in our society. Have you ever been fired or cursed by a cruel boss? We do it every week in the Great American Sports Complex, and those who pull the trigger do it to please us.

While it lasts, the community spirit of the cheering home crowd feels like friendship, and for a moment it is, until the game is over and we cannot think of what to say except to talk about more game. There is nothing wrong with game talk, but if that is *all* we have to say to each other, we are alone together again, shadows of the men we thought we were. It is not a stretch to say that the one-dimensional aspect of spectator entertainment contributes to the silence of men or that silent men "do" sports like they "do" church, all lined up like nice automatons. Except the games are usually more exciting, less judgmental, and they sell beer. Spectator sports *and* spectator church both have lethal power, but not the power to lead men closer to the kingdom of God.

WHAT A YOUNG BOY WANTS AND A GROWN MAN NEEDS

When a boy is young, game and story are two of the things most important in life — and both are connected to his identity. What child does not say to his father, "Come play with me," "Read me a story," or "Tell me what it was like when you were growing up." In the life of a child, this love of game and story is instinctive and nurtures what we celebrate about humanity. Game and story are two of the primary ways in which children connect with their fathers.

When fathers are missing or silent, it is more difficult for a boy or young man to discover his manhood. It is not easy for a young man to civilize or enlighten himself, and a healthy balance of game and story, rooted in the essence and presence of his father, is meant to help him on his way. The true narrative of a father creates a lifelong point of reference as a young man learns to create and tell his own story. This is so because a father's narrative includes for his sons, and in perhaps even more powerful ways for his daughters, a living portrait of his character, his work ethic, his love, his ability to create, his desire to serve, and his capacity to play. As a father, you are the nearest point of reference your children will ever have to what the words *Dad, man, husband,* and *father* actually mean during their formative years and throughout their entire lives. True narratives of fathers are not perfect pictures — they include honesty about sorrows and joy, failure and success, but a son does not need a perfect story or a perfect picture to gain from his father what he needs to develop into a healthy human being. He does, however, need a father, and he does need his father's narrative, or his life will become much more difficult than it was ever meant to be. Without him, a son is forced to travel a long and unnatural route to discover the great strength and tenderness of manhood. Sadly, some never do.

> **When fathers are missing or silent, it is more difficult for a boy or young man to discover his manhood.**

The needs of grown men are not much different from the needs of boys. Both enjoy a better life when game and story are held in healthy equilibrium. Game represents the lighter side of life — our humor and playfulness, our fascination with achievement and dedication to accomplishing what is above and beyond. It represents healthy competition, fairness, individual accomplishment, and the value of team, while playing by the rules to accomplish our goals. Game reinforces a stubborn suspicion that not *all* men are created equal, that our differences are important and serve as benefits for our greater good.

Story taps the root of who we are, the importance of *our* narrative, the unique elements of *our* design, and what we were created for by God. It communicates not only facts about us, but our essence as men, and reminds us of the intractable truth that all men are of equal *value*. Game and story elevate our character. Together they give us depth of field and perspective, and they write our history and create what we love when we say we love life.

Game and story elevate our character. Together they give us depth of field and perspective, and they write our history and create what we love when we say we love life.

By now you may think I grew up in a cultural bubble. I did. It was a stark yet pretty little world without television, a world not yet dominated by professional games. We could not have afforded a TV, and given the work and play required to make a family farm a place of peace and plenty, I have no idea when we would have turned the thing on. There was also the little problem that having a TV might be a sin, or at least a waste of time, which on the farm was the same thing as sin. I didn't have two relatives who would have disagreed. Mom and Dad always said their "live entertainment"—their kids—was better than anything on television, a comment that made us feel proud and safe. So, of course, when I got married at twenty-eight years old, my new wife had to inform me about American pop culture icons I had missed, such as *Leave It to Beaver*, *Ed Sullivan*, *The Brady Bunch*, and *Father Knows Best*. All these were lost to me while I learned that life is not supposed to be one, boring, global, homogenous puree. Fortunately, Dad bought a car with a radio that worked just in time to catch the tail end of early Beatlemania. The current farce, if I am a young man, is that I am to spend enough of my life in front of a screen or with a ball in my hand until I can no longer distinguish my reality from yours. I still feel a bit like Don Quixote living in a world that was once real and that asks me to believe what is before me is not imaginary.

I remember only three TV programs when I was a kid—a John Wayne Western, an episode of *Gilligan's Island*, and the funeral of Sir Winston Churchill. On the day of Churchill's funeral, I knocked on the door of a grumpy old-world immigrant who never answered his door. Because I heard his TV blaring, I was determined to knock until I got an answer. I was peddling Mom's famous homemade bread, confident I could make the sale. When the door opened, I was ordered to come in, sit down, and be quiet until the historic funeral march from Westminster Hall to St. Paul's Cathedral ended. The dissonant, wild bells of every church in London rang their dirge as an entire world in mourning paid tribute to Sir Winston Churchill, that "Last Lion." Thirteen years old, I left Mr. Wiggins's home enriched, only slightly more so by the two quarters jingling in my pocket.

Stories were what we lived for—stories at bedtime, story time in our little country schoolhouse after lunch where, from first through eighth grade, our teachers read books such as *Little House on the Prairie* and other classics. We heard stories of Christian martyrs who were distant relatives in Switzerland, stories of great-grandparents homesteading to Nebraska after the Civil War, and funny stories about Great-Granddaddy Glick, who insisted on having his leg amputated on the kitchen table because he did not want to pay the costs at the hospital. We listened to stories of crazy city folks from New York, of slaves and sharecroppers oppressed "down South," of practical jokes by the "three uncles," of barn fires and entire communities rebuilding a neighbor's barn in just a few days with freshly cut timber from the mountain. Such things we witnessed with our own eyes. We heard of near-legendary feats by clever heroes such as Abe Lincoln and Dad and all the other old-timers, and we loved Sunday afternoon stories told by visitors from near and far. Stories gave us something to think about, to aspire to, and to dream about. They expanded our worldview and made us wonder where the airplanes were going, and they gave us plenty to question and to admire.

Popular obsessions, unlike stories, tend to narrow a man's field of vision while promising the opposite. The history of wars alone, if we could learn from them, would instruct us in this. Does anyone want to guess whether the scenario of every person on earth having exactly the same gadgets will serve to enrich us? Ed, my sports-freak banker friend, who would lay down his life for me in a flash without a second thought, still does not have a cell phone, and I'll bet he is the only senior executive VP of a major regional bank anywhere in the world without one. This, of course, is how he funds his sports habit. For guys who have lost, buried, or not yet discovered their life narrative, sports are metaphors for life in which the contest in the arena represents their best conquest. These conquests, of course, are not life, but they have power and attraction in our society because they represent life and perhaps even a kind of lost purity. Ed could explain this to you.

FINDING OUR WAY OUT OF THE COLISEUM

God seems to be attracted to children and to men who become like children. We know he assigns guardian angels to each child, and Jesus scolded his friends who told kids to leave him alone. Grown-ups are not permitted, the Bible says, to enter the kingdom of heaven unless they become like children. So what's the deal with being told to grow up all my life?

Our refrigerator is plastered with pictures of kids all the time. Always has been. These cute little faces remind me of what my face should look like, of how my heart is reflected in my face. When I see their trusting little mugs, their soulful eyes, and their innocence, I am mesmerized by the words of Jesus to turn and become like children if we want to enter the kingdom of God. This is truth for big people. He wasn't joking, and so if we want to enter the kingdom of God, we're going to have to figure out what he meant and come gently to the grace he offers.

I recently made a new friend, whom I hope will be my friend for life — in this life and in the life to come. Her name is Gracie, and at the time we met, she was eight years old. My wife and I were having dinner one evening with her parents and our good friends, Jimmy and Tina. Gracie seemed at first like just another average child, busy with whatever it is that keeps children busy these days. But toward the end of the evening, she joined the adult conversation, and what a whistler she is. She and I talked for forty-five minutes about everything and anything — the life and poetry of Shel Silverstein, science, math, books, her favorite authors, her dreams, how she won her third-grade election for class president but refused to vote for herself because if she won, it would not have meant as much as her peers voting for her. She asked me questions about my life, my children, my work, my favorite books, and what I like to do. I am not sure that I have ever met a person more curious than Gracie. At one turn in the conversation, she gave me some good advice. With excitement rippling in her voice, she said, "This is important. Only you can be you, and you have to learn how to be you — and you're doing it." She spoke of her childhood as if it had both passed and was yet to come, and she told me about her friends and what they mean to her. At eight years old, she looked me straight in the eye, reading the nuances, tracking the conversation, engaging a man fifty years her senior. When the evening ended, she leaned forward and said, "This has been the conversation of a lifetime. Thank you." And so it was.

David, the sweet psalmist of Israel, wrote, "Deliver my soul ..., O LORD, from men of the world whose portion is in this life."[2] Men whose orientation is only in this life will mess up your soul and diminish your spirit if you are entangled with the mind-set that controls and drives their lives. This life is the best some men will ever have. These men have no reliable hope of heaven within them, no help from a Savior, no expectation of life after death, and no satisfaction at the end of their days that the life they lived was worth much of anything. Dust returning to dust, at the end, can take little confidence in itself.

How quickly a grown man can be reduced to a handful of dust and ashes. So if this life is the best they will have and no eternal inheritance awaits them, why should they not play away their days as best they can? I understand why such men take all they can get out of this life. Who would take less? A man who believes this life is the end of our existence rather than the beginning, who believes this life is as good as it's going to get, provides confirmation of the dying soul within him. The lilting song of the dead and dying, "Eat, drink, and be merry, for tomorrow we die," is sung by those for whom light, love, and the glory of hope have departed from their faces. Deliver my soul from them, the writer declares, for they are dead already. Seeing life come to a dead man, however, is quite the ticket, and I have seen it with my own eyes.

A man who has been reborn will tell you he has discovered and received free gifts that he did not earn or deserve. This declaration points to a spiritual change so dynamic and new it indeed has made the dead spirit within him alive. The order of magnitude is so great that Jesus described this change as becoming like children. All of us can remember childhood wonder and awe, the discovery of beauty, the warmth of trust, and the joy of early friendship before betrayal. We remember a cold glass of milk, the gladness of love oozing from hot chocolate chip cookies fresh from Grandma's oven, or the free-flowing tears of childhood when hurts needed a healing touch of love and mistakes needed mending. This is what Jesus wants in the spirit of a full-grown man — the simplicity, wonder, and pleasures of childhood, including the satisfaction of hot cookies and cold milk, coupled with the wisdom and insight of manhood.

Our memory of this phenomenon we call childhood and our longing for more of its purity are what God uses at the moment of our spiritual rebirth to help us receive by the faith of a child what we could not receive through our minds and adult experience alone. Invited to dwell within us in his spectacular fullness, God gives us life and invites us to join him in his magnificent kingdom. As many as receive him, to them he gives the right to become children of God. This testimony of John the apostle, who received the gospel of Christ directly from Jesus whose kingdom we seek, is what I know about Jesus and his glorious kingdom from firsthand experience. Free now to leave the earn-your-own-way matrix of the coliseum, I see joyful grown-up children, dancing their way into the streets of this world, on their way to the glorious kingdom.

CELEBRATING WHAT IS NEW

"Your gentleness made me great." These five words buried in the Psalms provide a brilliant meditation for men.[3] They are spectacular in their obvious contradiction and are not exactly a paradigm from the world of sports or twenty-first-century corporate culture. Two opposing concepts combine into one multidimensional image of manhood that goes missing in many of our assumptions about God and the men who follow him.

Has any gentleness within you been celebrated as greatness, rewarded with a raise or promotion in your profession, or been taught to you by other men who have discovered their greatness though the gentleness of God? You may not believe that God is gentle, yet gentleness makes the character short list of evidence of the presence of God. Consider how seldom you hear of this magnificent quality of life. Christian churches love to preach about the need for boldness — and they are not wrong for doing so — but boldness is not listed as evidence of *God's presence*. Jesus does not tell his disciples to go out and be bold for him. That would require an impossible religious performance outside the context of relationship with him. Having delivered them from earn-your-way performance religion, he does not then require them to live by such rules. He advises them, instead, to join him in the celebration of the bread and the wine, to wait for power from his Father, and to live as wise as serpents and as innocent as doves. Jesus wants men strong, wise, and gentle, apparently.

From our earliest moments on earth, we are taught to compete, to defend and demand our rights, and—if not given to us—to take what is rightfully ours. We envy most those who have accomplished great wealth or great success, yet we are always ready to envy the next chap who sets the new record. But the men we *admire* most and enjoy spending time with have many of these qualities: love, joy, peace, patience, kindness, goodness, faithfulness, gentleness, and self-control. The differences between the men we envy and the men we admire are not the slightest bit subtle. We appreciate our gentle Amish neighbors but do not actually think it would work very well for *us*.

Spectator sports and spectator churches have this in common: both elevate successful men and performance above other normal life qualities. Is this another example of what Jesus meant that "the kingdom of heaven has suffered violence"?[4] The kingdom of God is not like the kingdoms we create, nor is entering his kingdom based on performing high-octane feats or joining a dress-up-for-God club. In the peaceable kingdom, performance is set aside for a willingness to receive, and because receiving goes against our native philosophy of life, many men miss the benefits God has reserved for them. "I'm not going to take nuthin' from nobody" isn't going to work at the point of your need, and it certainly isn't something you hear coming from Jesus to describe life in his kingdom. That little illusive door through which one must pass, which requires receiving a gift instead of giving or earning one, is a stumbling block of enormous proportion to a self-made man or a self-centered church.

In the lexicon of our life together, we must exchange performance words such as *win*, *earn*, *success*, and *loss* for life-giving words such as *receive*, *accept*, *love*, and *celebrate*. The words by which our spiritual fathers invite us to participate in the life of Jesus at the table of his presence describe the prevailing way of life in his kingdom: "I also give to you that which I have received from the Lord." A man is set free to live when he realizes he cannot, and is not required to, give something he has not received, that the source from which he can receive is unlimited. Jesus embeds in his teaching this concept of a continual flow of life from God to man when he taught his disciples to pray, "Give us this day our daily bread."[5] We celebrate the kingdom as the gift of his *daily* presence.

Our stories are gifts we give to invite others into our presence. Every man has a story worth telling, but so many of us do not believe it and have not understood the benefit of passing along our stories to our kids or even to our friends. We've got to help our quiet brothers appreciate the unique beauty flowing in the narratives of their own lives. The hearts of our sons and daughters are like deep wells capable of running pure and clean for years, long after we are gone. Investing yourself and your story in your children causes the water in their wells to run sweet and clean. Native Americans knew how to restore a polluted spring and to keep the water pure, like fathers who invest their stories in their children.

How you tell your story is for you to decide, but I am sure you will rediscover something like the friendship you enjoyed with your childhood playmates as you begin passing along the bits and pieces of your life to those who are near and dear to you. If you have lost your playfulness or are obsessed by performance religion or your job, if you have made sports your idol, or if everything in your life is as serious as a terrorist attack, make friends with at least one truly literate and almost-balanced sports nut like my friend Ed, before you drive the rest of us crazy. Most *kids* don't think big people know how to have fun, so begin by telling or writing down for them memories of the fun you had as a kid. They'll ask the questions; you tell the story. In time, perhaps we can become men who, like Gracie, speak of their childhood as if it has passed and is yet to come.

FOUR

THE GLORY AND SHAME OF FATHERS AND SONS

In our fathers, we saw glimpses of you.
Prayer by David Moberg, "Dinner and Conversation" group

UNCOVER WHAT A MAN IS NOT talking about and you may just discover what he cares about most. My central premise, however, is that men aren't talking much about things that matter, and our silence is quite disturbing. But what you need to know about men is that they are more than willing to talk when they have the respect of those who are willing to listen, provided the topic isn't one more thing they really don't care about.

This became clear when our "Dinner and Conversation" guys met for an evening together in May. Our group got started after watching what happened when my friend BJ asked me to cancel my flight home from New York to help him with dinner for eight young men coming to his east side home. BJ has worked with men of all ages in the city for over twenty-five years and has learned to ask questions that get to the heart of what guys want to talk about. Questions at "Dinner and Conversation" range from "What gives you joy?" to "What is your deepest need right now in this season of your life?" That evening, after the normal dinner chatter, he asked each of the men to respond to one simple question: "What is the most surprising thing that has happened to you?"

Young men want to talk about that. Middle-aged and old guys

want to talk about that, and the conversation that night proved that young men, some of whom were sports heroes in high school and college, could talk about more than game. The evening ended with a sense of friendship among young men who would never have said what they did unless they'd been asked the right question.

"What was your father like?" I asked the men at one of our dinners. "Help us get to know you better by telling us about your dad." Men can talk all night about the things they really care about. That evening, seven guys talked about their fathers for more than three hours. That's something we really care about — who Dad is and was, what he did, what and whom he cared about most, and what memories we had of his love for us. Ask a man to talk about his dad in the company of other men who respect him, who will listen to him, and who will share their own stories, and you will find the deep wells of a man's soul.

Uncover what a man is not talking about and you may just discover what he cares about most.

That question led us to the headwaters where goodness, admiration, and joy are the tributaries of a man's soul. The admiration of our fathers also exposed profound longing for our fathers, thoughts about his and our inadequacies, and sadness. To a man, each of us expressed the wish we knew more about Dad — what he cared about, what he loved, how he made it through the hard times when he was our age, what he thought about us when we were young (Did he like me when I was a kid?), and what advice he would have for us today.

Three of our fathers were veterans of World War II. Two of those vets never talked about their experiences in that war, but when they died, their adult children found "a nondescript box" containing two treasures: love letters they exchanged with their wives during courtship and medals they received in the war. Both men had ten or more medals. We asked their sons why they thought their dads never talked about the war, and one said, "My dad was a pilot, and on D-Day his mission was to drop soldiers behind enemy lines. On that day, of the twenty or thirty men on each flight, sometimes only a few would reach the ground alive. Why would he want to talk about that? But the only things he kept until he died were those medals and love letters from his wife."

That's the way we are. We think about stepping between the bullets and our wives and kids. We think about rescuing our sons from the oncoming train, the passing truck, the threat of danger, large and small. We joke about sitting on the front porch cleaning our shotguns as we wait to meet our daughter's first date, but the thought behind the joke is dead serious. We work to keep the bill collector off our street, away from our front door, and we will not talk about these things in any place we will be derided or denigrated for how deeply we care. Raised eyebrows, the interruption of unimportant phone calls, a sharp word, a missed cue—these are enough for us to refuse to talk about how much we care.

During the course of that conversation, we discovered other things we had in common. Two men had great-grandfathers who homesteaded in Nebraska in the 1870s during the Nebraska Land Act. My Amish grandfather was two years old when his parents left home, family, and friends and headed west for the promise of free land and pioneer life on the American frontier. They lived on the prairie in a sod house for the first two years and scratched out a living for the next twenty years before returning home to the beautiful Kishacoquillas Valley in central Pennsylvania.

Our fathers, grandfathers, and great-grandfathers were stern men. The influences that steered them in that direction included devout religious faith that often embraced legalism instead of grace, the harsh existence of pioneer life, the Great Depression, two World Wars, and an unspoken obsession passed on to us that we would never again be poor. Talking about our fathers' characteristics at "Dinner and Conversation" helped us understand why they were so silent and why we tend toward silence in matters dearest to us. Some of those men discovered grace; others never did. One dad took care of his wife with Parkinson's disease for thirty-six years. That is grace, mercy, and love.

Sometimes our silence, as well as the silence of our fathers, is sin or caused by sin, but not always. Sometimes silence is wisdom awaiting an invitation to be heard. Men between the ages of forty-five and sixty are men between worlds, the old world and the new — between the pioneers and the iPods, the old man and the new man, the Adam and the Christ. When a guy stumbles into this season of life, he becomes uniquely aware of his location but

Ask a man to talk about his dad in the company of other men who respect him, who will listen to him, and who will share their own stories, and you will find the deep wells of a man's soul.

may not know where he is. He is somewhere he has never been. Actually, that's the truth no matter what age a man is, but at the beginning of the twenty-first century, it seems especially true for men whose near forebears helped pioneer the last great Western frontiers.

We are all sons, but we are called to be fathers, as Henri Nouwen says, and, at the end of our days, patriarchs. The words of Scripture remind us that "you do not have many fathers," indicating a difference between man's biological and spiritual office.[1]

Men sense that there was more in our fathers than we could see and are certain that there is more in us than we can now show our children. Understanding our inability to show ourselves to our children helps us appreciate why our fathers did not do so for us. Part of this is the cavalier yet benign thoughtlessness of youth that does not care to see while the seeing is easy. It becomes more difficult with aging fathers.

How could we know we would want to know more later, especially after our fathers were gone or their memories had faded or their ability to communicate became stultified? Their failure, and perhaps ours, has been in not passing along in words — spoken or written —

the virtue, the stories, the experiences, the pitfalls, and the wisdom that could have helped us understand our lives. Our fathers seldom shared their deepest personal feelings, doubts, and thoughts, and we have the same difficulty.

Even so, we all received something from them we cherish deeply. In spite of the distance from our fathers and the lack of communication, we did receive from them some of the essence of life, of manhood, of our identity and heritage. What we saw of our fathers in the glimpses they revealed about themselves inspired us for a lifetime, and the glimpse a man can see on this earth of his *heavenly* Father inspires him for eternity.

WITH THE ADMIRATION, LONGING ...

Longing for a father, by some design, is a universal human desire. Even if the longing is negative in every way—wishing our dad wasn't this, was that, kept his promises, wasn't so hard on Mom (make your own list)—we all have it. It takes years of absence and abuse by a father to turn this characteristic into complete apathy. I know many men who have never heard their fathers say, "I love you. I'm proud of you. You're the best son a dad could ever want," but the longing to hear those words never dies.

Longing for Dad—longing to know his wisdom, to discover who he was, what he cared about, how he got through the hard times, what made him the man he was—finds expression in his children, no matter their ages. Sometimes the loudest expression of a man's longings is his silence, and it is that silence in generations of men that turns the world, for many, into an orphanage.

We are like our father Adam after he sinned in Eden. He still had a Father but was cut off from his presence. What he had was memory of a Father and glimpses of him, but not his immediate presence. What he lost was both his Father's presence and communication with his Father, which could have provided guidance during the days of conflict with his sons, Cain and Abel.

This loss between Father and son created in Adam's sons the jealousies and avarice that led to the world's first fraternal murder. One found favor with God; the other did not. Both could have. One made a sacrifice acceptable to God; the other did not. One killed his brother and was a marked man for the rest of his life. A man's action against his brothers surely marks his life, just as his life is marked by things done against him. A wise father, however, could have helped both sons make an acceptable presentation to God.

We are like our father Adam after he sinned in Eden. He still had a Father but was cut off from his presence. What he had was memory of a Father and glimpses of him, but not his immediate presence.

Men feel something most of us cannot describe. It is a sense of being responsible for something we cannot control, for something we do not know. It's the condition of man described by distinguished professor emeritus of comparative literature and Italian at Indiana University Peter Bondanella, as "*homo claudus* (limping man), his wounds being the result of Adam's original sin."[*] We suspect our fathers knew something they could have told us but did not. Whatever it was they did not tell us, we wish they had. We see their limp, and we feel ours.

The result is that we do not know what to say to our sons and daughters. We cannot understand the purposes of our lives. We cannot explain why life becomes difficult and unpredictable. We know little about how to solve personal conflicts peacefully. We know how to start wars but not how to stop them. We do not know how to love our wives. We accept the responsibility of manhood, but we do not know what we are to do with it. We are "Adam again."

Many of our fathers are like that, and we are like them. We imitate what we know; we build what we can conceive—and nothing

---

[*] Quoted in Dante Alighieri, *The Inferno*, introduction and notes by Peter Bondanella (New York: Fine Creative Media, 2003), 4 (note 7, p. 182).

more. God, knowing this about man, gives us instruction to imitate the man Christ Jesus. Many men, while wanting to be like Dad in some respects because of great admiration for him, have determined to *not* be like him and to *not* be like the God of his fathers. We admire him, but he was not available, not present even when he was with us physically, to help us understand how to live. How little we were told of his struggles, his hard times, what he did to make it through. We admire him even more as we begin to discover the difficulty of our own struggles; while we seldom know how we will make it through, we admire Dad because he did. Still, we wish he had told us how, had given us advice and not waited for us to ask. Solomon writes, "The LORD reproves [instructs] him whom he loves, as a father the son in whom he delights."[2] A son wonders whether his father's silence means, somehow, that Dad did not—does not—delight in him.

> We suspect our fathers knew something they could have told us but did not. Whatever it was they did not tell us, we wish they had. We see their limp, and we feel ours.

After dinner with a friend one evening in Washington, D.C. (believe it or not, a conversation between two normal guys about fathers, sons, and our effort to understand ourselves as men—a conversation that lasted for hours), Don sent this note: "I do not exaggerate when I say that the condition of men accounts for the world being in the mess it is in. I have only a few clues as to why we find it impossible to connect with fathers, mentors, brothers, friends. I don't think I have lived a single day of my life for the past several years in which I did not long to have a wise, gentle old guy standing close by for advice. I recognize that my life is especially complex, but I think we all need that."

Here's what we know and what we did not hear from our fathers: We did not hear them say anything about their weaknesses until and unless they came bobbing up to the surface. Sons translate that into the idea that weakness is equivalent with shame. They showed us only their strength, and because of it we saw only half a man. No man who reveals only his strengths is showing his complete manhood. He is showing what he wishes were true, what he hopes will become true, but it is caricature and image, not the truth. Because of it we were cut off from good conversation and much wisdom, and we struggle now to learn what we should have been taught from adolescence. This is not about the adage that real men cry or don't cry; but by missing tears of any kind from our fathers, a truncated sense of reality develops within us. A boy doesn't know what is worth crying about. He assumes that not much falls into that category. The idea that a man's worth is linked to his strength or illusion of strength is powerful, and we are quite distracted with upholding the image that we are strong. Solomon writes, "The glory of young men is their strength, but the splendor of old men is their gray hair" — their wisdom.[3] But this text doesn't say anything about the process between youth and old age.

I was a strong farm kid from the country and the Pennsylvania backwoods, and no one could beat me (that was the image in my head). The truth is, I was strong and tough. I worked six days a week and more on Sunday, from before sunrise to late evening, planting and harvesting crops, operating our dairy, cleaning the stalls and cattle barn, fixing the fences, repairing equipment, and managing the family business. I enjoyed the glory of a young man's strength. As I grew older, while my body changed, my illusions did not. Then in 2002, and exactly one year later, during the last week of October, I took two severe falls, one while cleaning leaves off my roof, the other while riding a bike down the seventeen-mile Creeper Trail in southern Virginia. In both, my entire weight landed on my right shoulder. No bones broke, but the internal damage still plagues me. I faced physical weakness for the first time in my life.

There is a biblical paradox that falls hard in the mind of a man, but it is true: The strength of Jesus is made perfect in our weakness.[4] While the boast of a young man is his strength, the confession of an older man is: "I am a man of considerable weakness." An older man's confession is accompanied by a roaring laugh emanating from the deepest part of his soul, unless, perhaps, he has become bitter and has failed to discover laughter or the true language of manhood. Face-to-face with truth, a man must give up his self-illusion. Jesus replaces it with a dynamic reality. Hidden in a man's weaknesses are some of his greatest treasures.

In order for a man to pass through "the tough years" from strength to wisdom as his glory, he must undergo painful and sometimes bitter experiences. It took two physical falls and several of another kind for my life confession to change from "I am strong" to "I am weak, but God is strong." To become wise, a man must become broken, for the strength of wisdom is greater than physical strength. A young man seldom knows this, and if he is unprepared for the broken places of life, well, that is the crux of this book. Few men migrate well from one season of life to the next, and few older guys I know even have a language to explain what happened or is happening to them now. Young men tell me all the time, "No one in your generation talks to us unless they want something from us."

The more a man knows himself, however, the more he knows other men. The sooner a son realizes the similarities between his struggles and his father's struggles, whether they were spoken or not, the sooner he can come to peace with his past, his present, his future, and his father, whether living or dead. There is much to learn about our fathers and from our fathers. Frequently, there is also much to forgive. We have discovered as we have journeyed deeper into manhood that while there may be much about our fathers we must forgive, there is as much or more they must forgive in us. Through forgiveness, we can receive what we really need, which is healing, comfort, love, and

> **To become wise, a man must become broken, for the strength of wisdom is greater than physical strength.**

dynamic relationships with our fathers and other men, provided they are willing to enter into their own weakness to discover joy.

BEHIND EVERY PHYSICAL IMAGE, THERE IS A SPIRITUAL REALITY

The besetting sins of sons and fathers are the same, though the expressions of those sins may be demonstrated differently. In fact, the besetting sins of all men are the same, and to know this is the beginning of understanding and wisdom about men. The list of these sins can be found throughout the Scriptures. Or if you are not given to accepting wisdom from God and must learn everything the hard way, visit Las Vegas, Hollywood, Washington D.C., Amsterdam, Wall Street, or any street in the world, and observe the actions of men. Observe and then look to the thoughts that create the actions, and you will find the meaning. Or save yourself the expense and write down your own thoughts for one day, and you will discover how little separates you from all other men. The halls of power, the vault in the counting house, and the rooms of the brothel are part of the same building. The psalmist states that God looked down on the children of man to see if there were any who understood, who sought God—but there was not one.[5] God said to Moses he would visit the sins of the fathers on the children to the third and fourth generation if a man and his descendants would not repent of their sins and turn to him for forgiveness and healing.[6] This is not good news, but it is fair enough.

Some sons find themselves embroiled in certain sins and lifestyles their fathers never participated in. Gravity pulls hot lava downhill, and what starts out as fascination with evil in one generation flows toward full-blown addiction in the next. The modern idea that everything is the fault of someone else is bogus, but the idea that many sins are generational, handed down, learned as a way of life from parents, is true. A man can make his own choices, walk toward darkness, and find he has lost his way all on his own, or he can do it with friends. However he does it, he is by nature inclined to do so.

This is the spiritual gravitational force of our fallen nature, and the lure of self-fulfillment, self-gratification, and self-aggrandizement is powerful. Each man is responsible before God for his own sins and by participating in them makes an unspoken agreement with God to accept their going wages. Sin pays but has only one imperial currency—death, preceded by short-lived pleasures designed to take from a man only what is required for him to live; the rest he is allowed to keep if he can. He will soon discover that what he keeps, all he has left in his hand, is dust, straw, and ash, things that will neither sustain him nor be useful in rebuilding his broken life. God "repays to their face those who hate him, by destroying them. He will not be slack with one who hates him. He will repay him to his face."[7]

Jesus gives another twist of logic and truth when he said the Father did not send him to condemn the world, but that it was "condemned already" because it "has not believed in the name of the only Son of God."[8] Our flagrance and sin are self-condemning. Before this dismal news, however, comes the magnificent promise of God: "Know therefore that the LORD your God is God, the faithful God who keeps covenant and steadfast love with those who love him and keep his commandments, to a thousand generations."[9]

The beguiling thing about sin, all sin, is that it is not static, not benign, not inert. Unless a man understands the dynamic nature of the beast he fights, he will lose the battle, the war, and his life. No men who read this, except the very naive who believe they can master dragons they have not yet met, would disagree. The Bible offers a helpful profile: "Sin deceives." "Sin is crouching at the door." "Be sure your sin will find you out"—and much more.[10]

I have a wonderful relationship with my father, but it came at the cost of humility and honesty, something most sons do not offer to their fathers and many fathers withhold from their sons. With permission from my father to share part of our story, our mutual history, and our besetting sins, what follows may help you discover a key to healing in your family relationships and your relationships with other men.

For several years in my midtwenties, I lost my way spiritually, was completely isolated from family and friends who knew me, and did not have the encouragement of friends who were interested in the holiness of God. Quite the opposite. My friends were all looking for ways to be in the world and of it, while maintaining a form of Christian belief. Our mind-set was that since we held the right beliefs about Jesus, the cross, and traditional Christian doctrine, we could do just about anything we wanted. Demons believe the existence of God, and so did we. The unspoken question behind our actions, the same devilish question that trashed Adam and Eve in the garden of Eden, was: "Did God say . . . ?" We were wild, young prodigals, proud things who knew what they wanted and how to get it.

After several years of living with one foot in the flashing lights of the city and the other in the shadow of the church, God got my attention. He did so in a most dramatic way—an ex-farm boy with no friends and in serious debt, twenty-five years old, facedown in a barnyard. Even so, my sin caused me much shame, and I was unwilling to talk about it after that time of life-changing repentance. I was not only unwilling, but I did not know how to do it or know anyone I trusted enough to tell of it.

My honesty was still in its early stages, but at least it had begun. I was afraid my parents—particularly my dad—would find out, and I knew what I had done would be heartbreaking to my precious mother. What would Dad think? How would he handle the disappointment? Would I recover from the pain of his knowing? So I did what men do. I kept silent, for nearly twenty years.

During those decades of my life, I knew nothing of my father's personal nightmare. I saw him as nearly perfect. In short, what he was dealing with began in his teen years and plagued him into his midforties. He was desperate for God to help him. He tells me now that his prayers during that time were cries for help, but he told no one about his struggles. Not a pastor, not his wife, not a friend, not any of his eight brothers. He was alone, and he knew it. A gifted man, he believed himself to be disqualified from anything but the most menial service in the church.

When he was forty-six years old, he had a heart attack and was in the hospital for four weeks. A year later, when his doctor gave him the green light, he got back to farming, back on the tractor, and was planting corn in the spring when he had a second heart attack that put him in the hospital for another eight days. That was the end of his life as a farmer, but God spared his life and gave it back to him. Dad and I both believe those heart attacks, for which doctors could find no medical reason except stress, were blessings in disguise. God was answering his prayer for deliverance from his besetting sin. I will spare you the details; that part is Dad's story to tell.

Several more decades passed, and while Dad was able to conquer, by the mercy and grace of God, the outward expression of his sin, he had hurt someone years before, and it had to find the light of day. The sin found him out. The person he hurt, in a remarkable act of wisdom and grace, asked him to confess his sins. He did so in one of the most memorable experiences of our family life. Dad and Mom visited their seven children in four states while Dad told us his story, his history, his struggles, his sin. He did this while in his seventies, and God set him free.

God not only set Dad free, but his confession initiated a journey in my life and changed the way I live. I am not certain I would have had the courage to begin had he remained silent. One year later, I was riding with him in his pickup, and when we stopped, I asked him if we could talk. I mentioned his confession a year earlier. When I did, his shoulders slumped and his chin fell to his chest, his face full of grief and sorrow. I said, "Dad, a year ago you had the courage to confess your sins to your family. I would like to confess the sins of my youth to you." I don't think he could have been more shocked. We sat in that old truck and cried like men — real tears that conveyed real love and real sorrow. Sorrow and love flowed from our hearts, down our faces, into the sea of God's mercy. Our relationship was transformed.

There are simple steps any man can take toward freedom. If you are a father and have never told your sons and daughters you love them, do it today. Do it every day, no matter how old they are. Let your words and your actions combine into one consistent message, day by day, step by step. If you need to apologize to them for how you have hurt them, do it today. Be specific. Tell them you are sorry. Do not make it sound like it was really their fault, not yours, and don't say, "I'm sorry you felt that way."

One of the least explored concepts in relationships among fathers and sons is sharing burdens they neither can nor should carry alone. Good fathers are willing to bear great burdens for their sons, and sons, when they know they are loved, will do the same. Of this elegant kindness, George MacDonald wrote, "Then you see, my boy, how kind God is in tying us up in one bundle that way. It is a grand and beautiful thing that the fathers should suffer for the children, and the children for the fathers."[*]

If you are a father and have never told your sons and daughters you love them, do it today. Do it every day, no matter how old they are.

If you are a son with a father who cannot initiate such things, make the first move. Examine where you have hurt your father, dishonored or disrespected him, and begin with that. If he is dead or has disappeared and none of this is possible, talk to a close friend or another guy about it. I assure you he is dealing with or has dealt with exactly the same thing. And you must forgive your father from your heart for any hurts if you want your Father in heaven to forgive you. This is the incontrovertible law of God, and it is not open for change. Forgiveness is one of the greatest things you will ever accomplish. There is no other way for you to fully enjoy your remaining time on earth. Confession and

---

* George MacDonald, *Ranald Bannerman's Boyhood* (Philadelphia: Lippincott, 1871), 138.

forgiveness are your keys to life, to the fullness of your manhood, and to making life the adventure God designed it to be for you. As one old boy put it, with tears flowing down his smiling face, "I am so glad that God allowed me to live long enough to repent."

FIVE

OUR NEED FOR HELP

The lower we go in the scale of creation,
the more independent is the individual.

George MacDonald, *Paul Faber, Surgeon*

IT IS REMARKABLE THAT A MAN can lie in a gutter with his pride intact, unwilling to ask for help—especially not the kind of help he really needs. Self-sufficiency may be the least expected visible trait in a man who has lost it all, but pride is the last of the vices to die. Your gutter may be metaphorical or real, but if you're in it, now might be the best time to ask for a little help.

It's a sad fact of life that someone close to you is more likely than a stranger to hurt you. A parent is the most likely person to ruin a child. A man's most trusted friends and associates are the ones most likely to betray him in a business deal. At the heart of these rotten deals and wrecked relationships, arrogance and ignorance about how to solve basic human problems rule. *Asking* for help or forgiveness seems like an idea from a lost and forgotten culture. A father refuses to admit to his son he was wrong, and the son learns he should never admit his own wrongdoing. A friend hurts his brother but thinks he cannot go to him with openness and honesty about his failure since he has no guarantee he will be met with the same.

Men must learn to approach other men with a strong yet gentle grace. They should be taught by fathers or older men when fathers are absent. Without such a commitment to honesty and resolving the most basic human problems, the friendship ends, the business deal dissolves, and two more men walk away from each other into isolation or bitterness, intent on never being hurt in that way again. Import these charming weaknesses into marriage, and a man can soon expect the beloved wife of his youth to curse the day she said "I do."

Like many gifted men before and after him, Ernest Hemingway, our great American writer, found within himself a powerful force of nature, a driving quest to cast and uphold the self-made image of himself as a man's man. His biographers can tell you more precisely the elements of his formation as a writer and his journey from childhood to manhood, but I believe his adult life was a quest for spiritual meaning. Although Hemingway's was not the quest of a Christian or even that of a philosopher, who could dismiss his life as something less than a legitimate search for significance? His life, in the best and worst ways, almost perfectly resembles the lives of many men.

Hemingway's life and work define a man in struggle. He was a writer, a hunter, a ladies' man, a fighter, and a connoisseur of life—an inebriated observer within an existential moment. His dominant themes were man taming nature, man confronting God, man triumphing over man, man against death, and man conquering and controlling his own destiny. He was a depressed soul, haunted by his own depression.

In Hemingway one sees a visceral beauty, raw honesty etched with despair, genius obscured by blindness, a sense of man as master of his own fate yet prisoner of his own limitations. He leaves his reader hungry and hopeless, a consequence of his own appetites and despair. Consequently, Hemingway and other male writers contributed to twentieth-century concepts of manhood a refinement of the art of boredom, a glamorization of personal conquest without purpose, and a renaissance after World War I of rugged individualism cast as the true American spirit. He celebrated the ideal of man as an island unto himself, yet perhaps unwittingly also pulverized that ideal under his skillful pen.

Hemingway offers the best that man alone can achieve. He won battles, but never a war. His enjoyment of relationships was followed by fragmentation and desertion. Reckless sexual pursuits left an abiding emptiness. In his physical conquests, neither fighter nor hunter was fulfilled by the kill. John Steinbeck, in a letter to Pascal Covici in July 1961, wrote of Hemingway's death: "I find it shocking. He had only one theme—only one. A man contends with the forces of the world, called fate, and meets them with courage.... A little like Capa [the famous *Life* photographer], he created an ideal image of himself and then tried to live it."* Some classic literature, descendants of a few hundred cats in Cuba and Key West, a skeleton, some old photographs, and the lesson of Hemingway's life are all that remain. "Suicide man" has destroyed "man's man."

IS THAT ALL THERE IS?

Hemingway was not created by God to become the whipping boy of moralists. His life and writings provide a valuable chronicle, which is, to some degree, a documentation of the soul of every man who proposes to live "on the grid" of self-sufficiency. Perhaps he has documented your life, and spiritual and emotional suicide may create results as devastating as physical suicide for those close to you.

In the West, we live in a world where significance and meaning have become our civil and inalienable rights. Are they not, in a Constitution somewhere, guaranteed to us? We become sure of this very early in life. A young man can hear the parental mantra in his sleep: "Study hard so you can get good grades so you can get into a good college so you can graduate and get a good job." So he does. He graduates from college, secures his first job, buys a car, gets an apartment, and goes to work. He pays his rent and makes his car payments, and he parties on the weekend and any other night he can find a party. He does this for two or three months or a year until he utters an awful

---

* Quoted in "The *Paris Review* Interviews: The Art of Fiction No. 45: John Steinbeck," Fall 1975.

question he never thought he would ask: "Is that all there is?" This is the same haunting question asked by millions of men at the end of their lives, by scores of athletes after their highest achievements, or in the silence following the roar of the crowd in the last game.

For the young man asking this question, this can be the beginning of death. Work hard to pay off the college debts or the debts from frivolous living—or both—or work hard to support that cute, young wife. Or work hard just because that's what men do, because it fills a primal need of man to provide for his family. This is the season in which most guys quit talking to other guys about the things that trouble them (if they haven't done so already). Who has the time or energy left after a long day at work to talk about the things that count, or to talk at all? There's just enough time left in the weekend to go to a game, cut the grass, have dinner with family or friends, perhaps go to church or sleep in, or flip on the computer or TV for a quick fix. Like a dream, the weekend is over, and it's back to work we go.

Years go by, and soon, for many men, life is all about performance, figuring how not to fail at work or in one or more significant relationships. We tell ourselves we'll figure it out soon, but we don't talk about it.

I talked to a young friend recently, a life-of-the-party guy, who, six months into his first real job after graduate school, could not believe how little meaningful contact he has with other men. Multiply that six-month period by eighty or a hundred, and you have the entire lifetime of a man's working years. Ask older men how they did it, how they just kept working year after year, and most will say, "I don't know. I did what I had to do. I just never thought about it, I guess."

But what happens if you do think about it? What happens if you are awake? What happens if you are not willing to participate in a mass emotional and spiritual death march for men? Or drink yourself into oblivion? Or divorce the wife of your youth? Or submit to addictions more powerful than yourself? Or pretend you are the only guy on the planet smart enough to avoid the pain of life? Or live without the company of men?

What about *you*? And what happens if all the bad stuff has already happened or is starting to happen to you? How do you stop *that* runaway train? Just when you thought you were smart enough to be the judge of others, as Francis Schaeffer said, you discover your own words and actions are enough to condemn you.[*]

Come, then, inside the quiet world of men — a world of insatiable appetites driven by lost dreams, by disappointment in relationships, by failures and the other things you seldom, if ever, have heard older men in your life talk about. A man feels the dark hunger fueled by the silence of the heart before external signs of starvation appear. And when a man defines his life by his performance, his very criterion for success becomes his personal power train to disaster.

> **When a man defines his life by his performance, his very criterion for success becomes his personal power train to disaster.**

Most guys are fairly bright, and the default setting in a guy's mind says, "If no one ever talks about this, I must be the only man in the world to ever have this problem. I must be the only guy in the church this messed up, the only guy in my family this stupid, the only guy at work so badly wrecked." When a man's heart is dead, the default settings of the mind are often indistinguishable from the lies of the Devil.

A friend of mine says, "Men don't just have issues; we have the whole subscription." Men love to talk about philosophy, theories, probabilities, and speculations. Men want to talk about the *problem* of divorce, as one writer put it, while the women want to know how the wife and children are getting along. Until men get honest with each other, when we talk about our issues, it's likely to be 99 percent theory, a practiced word dance around the sorry facts.

Men may talk about the *problem* of pornography, while up to 50 percent of the men in the conversation struggle with perversion or are

---

[*] Francis A. Schaeffer, *The Finished Work of Christ* (Wheaton, Ill.: Crossway, 1998), 45–47.

stone-cold sexual addicts. No word about that, of course, no admission of personal need, and little discussion of content that lasts more than sixty seconds! Time for more sports chatter, a favorite shell game with men. Problems in the abstract are fair game, as are past personal problems. Men seldom talk deeply about their current struggles and insecurities or admit their own spiritual coldness and the distance they feel from God at that very moment. A man's fear of exposure is titanic.

Blame the preacher, blame your wife or the lousy kids God gave you, blame your business partners, blame the government, blame dumb luck, or blame the wall you bang your head against. Men who live in isolation or in shame-based environments seldom accept responsibility for their own choices. Blaming oneself is not the same as accepting responsibility, nor is it the means of grace by which you will find healing. The good fish are not in the shallows; the proof is not in the theory.

> **Blaming oneself is not the same as accepting responsibility.**

DESTROYING THE POWER OF SECRETS

Listen to another kind of male conversation: The pastor says, "Guys, I struggle with sex and want more than my wife thinks any man should want or need, and far more than I can expect my wife to give me. I can't resist the desire to watch a sexually explicit show unless I'm honest about my struggles. Can any of you men relate to that, or am I the only recuperating sex freak in the room?"

A traveling artist friend says, "I refuse to travel alone, because the urge toward perversion and the loneliness of being on the road are more than I can take. When I am alone, I am constantly on the hunt for sexual content. In fact, my sideman often comes into my room and tapes a sign on my TV that reads, 'I will set no vain thing before my eyes.' That helps."

Another man, a respected community leader, says, "I am a recovering racist, and I struggle not only with people of other ethnic origins but with people of different political persuasions, with the poor, with men who are HIV positive, with women who expect me to treat them as equals. I'm growing, but I want my brothers to know that I have a long way to go. Please pray for me."

Another brother says, "I have a good business and the ability to make more money than I need, but I am not a generous man. I am stingy, self-satisfied, and self-indulgent by every definition of those words, and I am here to say the nice church member facade you see is a lie. I take advantage of people, and I need help."

Everything gets quiet for a little while. All the guys in the group know there's little reason left to hide. So the church bully (most churches have several) says, "I have such a horrible ability to offend people. I analyze everything that moves, and I can't keep my mouth shut about what's wrong. I can only say this morning that I am the most arrogant person I know. I am so empty, so lonely, and so sorry, and it may take a long time to learn what I need to learn. I hope you guys don't give up on me."

The last guy in the room says, "I treat my wife worse than I would treat my enemy. I want to love her, but I no longer know how to express my feelings or the fact that I don't feel much at all. Sometimes I'm not sure I can go on. I'm a wreck of a husband, and our family is a disaster."

Get a couple of guys to try that in your circle of friends. Sounds like pure fiction, right? It's not. It's possible. You'll either start the first great awakening of the twenty-first century or be placed in solitary confinement.

Sadly, most men's groups don't even come close to being honest. Prayer requests are made for other people — my wife's relatives, for example. Or we'll say, "I know we're not supposed to pray for the Yankees to win again, but could we pray for safety and a good time at the game?" We may as well be praying for the healing of marriages of characters in the daytime TV soaps.

The biblical writer urged, "Confess your sins to one another and pray for one another, that you may be healed."[1] Funny. Confess, pray, and be healed? Most of us think all we need is forgiveness, another chance, and we won't mess up again, but we actually do need to be healed as much as we need to be forgiven. In Christ, if I'm reading this right, we're already forgiven. Done deal, but we're not healed, deeply healed, without confession.

LEGALISM CAN'T HELP YOU

There's an idea floating around that God requires men to participate in a small group that will provide accountability for the men in the group. We even have a crummy little legalistic name for them: accountability groups. It *could* be good for you to belong to a men's group, but it would be silly to make the group responsible for something it cannot do. I was in such a group once, and we discovered the hard way that none of us could even ask each other for help. You could say we found a way to be connected in surface friendships, but we were deeply entrenched in our own gutters.

In Christ, we're already forgiven. Done deal, but we're not healed, deeply healed, without confession.

Within about two years of "becoming accountable," the whole thing fell apart. Unaware of what was happening deep within our brothers, our group suffered every kind of unresolved inner conflict you should expect from partially honest men. Since the sins of men are the same, ours need no further broadcast here (think of what you would do if you were left alone too long), but they were dark, often sexual, and rooted in long histories of shame, disassociation, and guilt. Our group failed because we had no idea how to develop friendships that could have anchored our hearts in reality and truth. We reached middle age without the tools needed to navigate, and the boats we were in developed leaks and sank before we knew we were going down.

After one of the brothers "fell off the porch," the church sent a gentle posse to find him. To his credit, he did not run away, although the inclination to do so must have been very great. He did not run away, but he faced his family and friends and began a very long walk toward healing and restoration. I have wondered whether I, in the same situation, would have run and hid, especially from the specter of my own behavior.

Meanwhile, I sat alone in the now very small men's group wondering what in the world had just happened. In my despair, I was like the psalmist, who wrote, "All men are liars."[2] I began to believe that all men are liars, and if it is too much to say that I began to hate my brothers, I certainly distrusted them. Our experiment in sharing life, on the surface at least, ended in abject failure — that is, if you believe revealing hidden sin is something other than the work of the Holy Spirit. Except for one brother, who agreed to be sent away for help, our small group was not very accountable and not terribly honest. Our group certainly was, on the other hand, small.

Here's what I think happened. To a man, all our wives were thrilled that we would meet each week in our "Porch Group" for prayer, fellowship, and Bible reading. Is not that supposed to be enough? Apparently it is not. Three out of four guys do *not* fall off the porch if that is enough.

Each of our wives was thrilled for a second reason: we were being accountable to each other. What they could not tell was that ours was a pose, unintentional as such, but a pose all the same. We received our weekly religious Botox shots and looked better, but what we needed was heart surgery.

While the real purpose of our group seems to have been God's plan to reveal our disease and lack of authentic friendship, the idea that we were an "accountability group" was a farce, one existing in at least four dimensions.

The first is that it *appeared* to be an accountability group. Every wife knows her husband has issues and needs to talk with other men but seldom does. The assumption about men's groups is that men actually talk in them about our own crap. Most of the time we do not, but the wife breathes a sigh of relief because it looks likes her man has friends and is finally talking. The first farce is an outright deception.

The second farce about accountability groups is this: No man can tell whether his brother is being honest or not. Even if he is being completely honest, which is doubtful, each man is in control of what he will do when the meeting is over. Controlling a man's behavior never changes his heart. Control freaks, take note.

The third is that no man can actually hold another man accountable, even if both men want the other to do this for him. Accountability is the work of the Spirit of God, not of men. I've begun to wonder if the word *accountability* is even in the Bible. Someone with a concordance, look that up, please.

The fourth and most damaging is that what men should be learning to discuss with other men is shoved deep into the recesses of the heart, to the place where lies are kept and fed — or what should be discussed with one's wife is brushed over with other men and never mentioned to his wife.

What is the link between Hemingway, our porch, and you? It is this: Finding a man as honest as Hemingway is rare. It is a battle to not give in to discouragement and depression. No man wants his dreams to die, his passion to dissolve, his purpose to be lost, his illusions about himself shattered. What may have pushed Hemingway over the cliff, not being able to return to his beloved Cuba after the Bay of Pigs invasion, seems like a mere feather touch. In the dust of lost dreams, it does not take much to destroy a man, and apathy almost feels like real peace.

Controlling a man's behavior never changes his heart.

NO VOICES — JUST *ONE* VOICE

While a man may be silent, a man's inner world is filled with many voices. There are voices from the past offering regular profit-and-loss statements on a man's self-worth; voices of a parent, a teacher, or a fallen hero; the childish schoolyard voices of bullies and mockers. Every man can remember the vivid, burning shame he felt as these voices first etched his tender, boyish heart. There are the legalistic voices of failed religion, competitive voices of performance and power, siren voices of materialism, and voices that win lost arguments in the screaming silence of the mind. Sometimes there are voices of a wife or a mother who does not understand the importance of her words, or who does understand but doesn't care what is damaged when she speaks. What shatters is his sense of self-worth; what breaks is his heart.

Other voices may be those of friends or business partners, who, for the sake of profit or fame, betray loyalty and friendship with the line, "We still want to be friends, but we just don't want to do business with you anymore." Or worse yet, "We think our friendship will be stronger if we quit working together," the last words you are likely to hear from them. You may have done the same, and if so, you can't be feeling great about what you said or why you said it. Your careless or angry words may be the recording played over and over in the mind of your ex-friend.

Either end of betrayal is the dirty end of the stick, but most of the voices you hear inside have to do with what you fear, or they identify a prison in which you are incarcerated due to your unwillingness to forgive the offenses committed against you. This legion of voices continues throughout a man's life until he learns to listen and follow the one voice that matters.

My wife and I were playing a game recently with our daughter, her husband, and several friends. It was my daughter's turn to roll the dice, and when she did, the group erupted with shouts and advice about what she should do. The noise was deafening. Our enthusiasm was unabated until she looked at us and commanded quietly, "No voices." The room fell silent, and she proceeded with her own decision, which led to her winning the game.

I don't know about you, but the voices in my head can ruin a perfectly good weekend. It does not take much. A competitor gets an edge, and I play over and over the moment when I missed my opportunity. My wife and I may have an argument, or someone says something I can't let go of, or I worry about what someone may think regarding something I did or said, so I dive into the pool of voices until I nearly drown in their pity, their anxiety, their fear, their accusations, and their conceit. The voices can make a man miss a bluebird sky, a smile, or the tug of his son's hand begging him to "come play with me." The voices prove constantly the need to "be still, and know that I am God" and to "let not your hearts be troubled."

To be healthy in your relationships with God and with people, learn to distinguish good voices from bad so you can reject those that repeat only worn-out lies from the enemy of your soul. If you listen to lies from the past and the present, or even lies you tell yourself, stop it. Commit from this day forward to accept only truth. You have to commit to live in truth, to love it, and to follow it wherever it leads. I hear the good and familiar voice of my son reminding me, "Truth is enough." Being a man, the kind of man *you* respect, begins with accepting the truth about yourself, and then moving forward.

If you have been living or hiding in a lie, seeking the truth about yourself will seem like self-betrayal, especially if you have separated yourself from reality with addiction. Self-truth will actually feel like your best friend has betrayed you. If so, you need a better friend! Finding the truth about you is an act of worship because it is an act of obedience. You must be willing to jettison self-pride before truth will set you free. The way of the cross first brings you face-to-face with reality so you can see the beauty God created in you and for you, before you can see the completed man of God you will one day become. This is the order of all things true: first the cross, then reality, then freedom, and then an astonishing view of what is yet to come.

Any voice that is not in character with "the voice that breathed o'er Eden," as John Keble wrote in a hymn, must be sent away forever.

Tuning out other voices telling you what you are and what you are not, what you will become or what you will not become, what you are worth or that you are worthless, is essential if you are to ever find your own voice. This does not mean you do not listen to your wife, your friends, your children, or the counsel of other men. Just check what they say by the Holy Spirit and the Word of God. Finding your own voice, in fact, will help you become a better listener. Imagine that! Finding your voice and bringing your voice into character with God actually help you discover the joy of manhood as God meant it to be.

It is written that "the righteous shall live by faith," and in the end, without faith a man cannot live at all, as Hemingway proved.[3] Without faith, the one thing left to do is die, to fulfill the truth of the lie by which faithless men order their lives.

If all this sounds right to you, but you are weak in faith, the Scriptures teach us that "faith comes from hearing, and hearing through the word of Christ."[4] Listen to the one and only Voice who can ever help you hear. Start by hearing God's Word. Read the Scriptures aloud to yourself everyday. It is impossible to remain weak in your faith if your heart, soul, and mind are hearing the Word of God and if you are daily asking God by his power to reveal his truth to your heart and mind. Ask him to help you every five minutes, if that's what it takes to come to understand and accept his grace and goodness. In other words, make accepting truth by faith your number one priority.

> **To be healthy in your relationships with God and with people, learn to distinguish good voices from bad so you can reject those that repeat only worn-out lies from the enemy of your soul.**

I end this chapter with a few observations about a man's performance, which, incidentally, often stems directly from the presence of voices (or absence of appropriate voices) that have created expectations within him so that he may not be able to separate himself from his own performance. Some of our greatest American entertainers have confused their person and their performance. Many of them had parents who did not tell them they are loved for who they are or gave them compliments only if their performance merited one. I once represented a brilliant comedian who said he never once heard his father say, "I love you." So he turned to the applause of his audience for the substitute, to his audience as to a therapist, and then to other, more damning vices. Men who have difficulty separating what they do from who they are may

Men who have difficulty separating what they do from who they are may be the least capable of asking for help.

be the least capable of asking for help. Sure, a man may be able to lead his company to greatness, but if performance is his number one priority, hiding his weaknesses is bound to be a close second.

IF WHAT YOU DO IS WHO YOU ARE ...

What follows is what I have learned by observing my own weaknesses and in my own career over the past twenty or thirty years of watching what men do to succeed while ignoring the issues of their own hearts. If what you do is who you are:

- expect to have a major life crisis by midlife or earlier; if you're really tough — and you probably are — there's a 100 percent probability you will not escape the pain awaiting you.
- expect that no matter how much you do, it will never be enough; this will be the curse of the standard you have set for yourself.
- expect shallowness in relationships.
- expect — when you least expect it — to experience an overwhelming sense of emptiness immediately following your greatest achievement.
- expect to react by denying the real causes for how you feel.

- expect to work even harder.
- expect to miss the riches of God's generous grace until you crash and burn.
- expect performance to become the cruel taskmaster of your life.
- expect to miss the really important things God has created for you.
- expect to not be able to feel God's love for you.
- expect a diminishing sense of self-worth and self-respect.
- expect to ask why you never see God doing much of anything anywhere anymore.
- expect isolation and alienation from those you love most.
- expect to love things and use people rather than to love people and use things.
- expect to actually want to remain bitter rather than become open and honest about your pain.
- expect a hard and sour end to your life.

If you decide to become a new man who willfully rejects performance as the measure of his worth, pray and never stop praying that Jesus will do whatever it takes to make your heart tender and new and to replace your messed-up life with something new and alive. Do that, and expect a fresh sense of what it means to be a man in such a dynamic way you may even come to think, for the first time in your life, that you are a man. Trust truth, and believe that the cost of shattered self-illusion is a price worth paying, that God can make you the man he designed you to be. It is his will to grant you your place among men. *That* is worth talking about. The choice is yours.

SIX

THE POWER OF OPPOSITES

IF YOU'RE ONE OF THE GUYS who says, "My wife is my best friend," I have to tell you I'm a little worried—and when I question this, I'm not intending to be negative in the slightest. Part of it is the wiring. We're just different. Not that it might not be true, of course, but if you really want me to believe you can tell her everything on your mind, I'll tell you to stop abusing her and go find a friend who can handle it, because I promise you, she cannot. A best friend, however, can.

Not far from our home, there is an old city dump known as "Bordeaux." How such a nice name got associated with the city dump is a shame, but the point is that men should not treat their wives like our city has treated Bordeaux. They were not created by God to be the dumping ground for all our crap. For example, try telling your sweet new wife that you are attracted to a pretty girl at work. Try telling her this when she is pregnant, and you'll find out exactly what you cannot say to your "best friend." You'll forget about it overnight, but she'll remember it until the day she puts your body in the ground. I recommend you treat your wife like the French care for *their* Bordeaux—and not like your personal garbage dump.

Men and women are different, to say the least, and if this topic doesn't get a good conversation started, I'm not sure what will. Ask a man to describe our intrinsic differences, and you're in for a few chuckles. Women just roll their eyes. The differences run deep and are beautiful—or not—depending what we make of them.

Some of my friends say busy women are no better at getting help for themselves than men, but I'm not so sure. Women seem to be more natural at it, have more available resources, and know how to find the help they need. Believe it or not, most of us guys are stumped on how to ask, are embarrassed that we need help, or don't have a friend close enough to trust with our deep and sometimes dark interiors. Requesting help for others is no problem, but asking for me is almost unthinkable. When God created us, it was pretty clear. Eve, the mother of all women, he said, would be a helper suitable for Adam—but I doubt Adam even knew the kind of help he needed. Half the time, neither do I. But Eve must have known, and my wife does too, and while this can include physical help, it is primarily emotional and spiritual help that we need. Wives have an uncanny sense to know what we need, whether or not we can put words to it. Women also have social networks and care systems that seem to grow easily among themselves. Men seldom do.

If men seem more suited for rigor and hard physical labor, a gift that comes with a certain dulling potion, women, as a class, are more naturally soft, nurturing, and intuitive. Women have inherent gifts and abilities men only dream of, and if they live in an environment of kindness and love, they will do almost anything to help us. Their God-given gifts include a highly sensitive BS meter; they know before we do when we're full of it. That women are willing to invest so much time and energy into our improvement is astonishing. For any man to believe that women were created to assume servile roles in relationships, marriage, and society is lunacy, the kind of lunacy only selfish men invent, and proof enough that evolution isn't exactly working.

MEN NEED MORE THAN THEMSELVES

Women may indeed be the more gifted and healthier half of the human race. God made it clear that a man needs a woman just to be normal. The first thing God said was "not good" about his creation was man's being alone; he said no such thing about women. Left alone too long or enslaved by figments of their own imaginations, men turn into the psychological equivalent of scorpions—you know, those silent and deadly predators who are more anthropoid than human at one end of the scale, or whiners, manipulators, and liars on the other. Seldom do they become balanced, well-adjusted men.

I was in New York on a rainy September evening, and my dinner guests had a last-minute schedule change. So I was sitting alone in a little Italian café on East 34th Street thinking, listening to the chatter of conversations, and enjoying a plate of ravioli. Two old boys, one well past his prime and the other only a few steps from the loading dock of the mortuary himself, were in an animated conversation about women. (Some topics for men, thankfully, never lose their charm.) I tuned in as the younger guy told his friend about a woman he was dating.

"No kidding," the old man said. Approval and envy lit up his tired face.

"Oh my god, no! I never lie," his friend said, "except to my wife."

What a commentary about himself, his wife, his mistress, and his friend—and one of those peculiar scenes that reflects more about the human colony than we wish to admit.

Women have a designed-by-God ability to help men get to the truth, as well as an impressive and devious capacity to use it against us because of a close encounter with a snake in a garden. And so, if you are a man with an interest in becoming the person God intends you to be, it is in your best interest to live with nothing to hide, and the woman you marry must know that the boss isn't her and it isn't you. In fact, you both must be straight on that little detail. In the hard days of marriage—which will come—you really can survive if you drill down to the character that makes it possible for you to bend your knees, not only in humility before your spouse, but also in the presence of God. But you're also going to need your friends, guys who can look you straight in the face and love you right where you are. Best friends don't let their brothers wander down the destructive road of knowing what is good and right and true but intentionally doing the opposite, and neither do caring wives.

So here we go, youthful masters of our own destinies, headlong into life and marriage with barely a clue about what comes next. Once the honeymoon is over and real life begins, husbands and wives discover quickly just how different they are — and how selfish. Add a few energetic kids and a couple of worn-out parents to the mix, and you may not even recognize yourself. A cartoon we came across soon after our second child was born summed it up this way: "One is hard, two is concrete." Thankfully, this isn't true *all* the time. Even so, the early years of marriage are a time of vibrant self-discovery, some of it difficult to make sense of. If you keep your heart and your love alive, the transformation you will experience is no less remarkable than the day you took your first step or spoke your first word. The words and steps you take together are like a great awakening, a journey begun, a new language of the soul.

In the hard days of marriage — which will come — you really can survive if you drill down to the character that makes it possible for you to bend your knees, not only in humility before your spouse, but also in the presence of God.

WHAT STRENGTHENS YOUR MARRIAGE AND WHAT MAKES IT WEAK?

Our "Dinner and Conversation" brothers met together one hot summer night, and the conversation was about marriage. "What makes your marriage strong," I asked, "and what makes it weak?" The very first answer: "Laughter." "When we laugh together," one guy said, "I forget about my need to feel significant, and she forgets about her need to be noticed." The evening was brilliant, as we, like elders sitting at the city gates talking about life, enjoyed the evening breeze. The weaknesses that diminish our marriages, we said, include being apathetic, trying to make our relationship perfect instead of helping it grow, engaging in perversion of any kind, breaking of intimacy, not engaging in dialogue, hearing but not listening carefully enough to remember, falling into routines that work against vitality, not being devoted to prayer, putting our jobs first, finishing our wives' sentences, being hampered by the habits and jaded life attitudes that were formed in us before we ever met, and trying to shape our wives into reflections of ourselves. One brother said, "We married not only each other but our histories, and it was almost too much to scale. Thank God we did."

To talk about what strengthened our marriages was equally fascinating, not only because of what was said, but also because not one of the sixteen guys around the table remembered a conversation with other men like the one we were having. "My wife and I did a timeline of our entire thirty-year marriage," one man said, "and reviewing everything we had survived blew us away. It helped us see ourselves less as victims and more as partners." Their marriages were strengthened, others said, by their histories of intimacy and mutual support, keeping each other honest with gentle truth, their similarity of social and theological views, their humility and openness to mystery, and "chasing her around like I'm still a teenager." "Working through the tough times," one said, "has matured us together." Believing in each other, being "stuck with each other," developing interests apart from the kids, deciding how much is enough, knowing where we are spiritually, keeping "the spark alive," inviting the presence of the Holy Spirit, and celebrating our differences are all significant in keeping our marriages moving in a positive direction. The fact that God made us male and female ought to give us a clue he's not afraid of conflict.

LEARN TO CELEBRATE YOUR DIFFERENCES

The distinctions between my wife and me are obvious, and I'm not sure we could be any more different. She is beautiful, and I'm quite average. She is talkative, an imaginative storyteller, and I'm more naturally quiet. She can tell a joke, while I can't remember a punch line to save my life—except one about Sir Winston Churchill that is pretty good. She's Irish and Swedish and maybe a few other things, and I am a stubborn Swiss-German. We're still searching history to see whether the Germans ever fought the Irish, or the Swiss the Swedes, just to find out who wins. I grew up in a home where we never fought, where neither Dad nor Mom ever raised their voices in anger. She grew up in a home where the person who threw the soup against the wall first won the fight. Mine was a conservative Amish and Mennonite heritage; hers was an assortment of drunk pagans—nice, but drunk. (Her family reunions were always held next to breweries.) I am from the East Coast, and she is from the West. I'm a country boy; she's a city girl. Richard, our hillbilly preacher friend from West Virginia, calls her "a California hot-tub Christian." Opposites attract. We fell in love. And that's when the fun began.

Linda was determined to teach me to fight, if only to find out what I am really thinking and to get me to actually say it. Being the third child in a solid row of boys, I know much about compromise and how to get what I want by negotiation and finding the middle ground. Seeing the other side

The fact that God made us male and female ought to give us a clue he's not afraid of conflict.

of a problem comes easily for me, but fighting was a whole new game. A few days into our marriage, soon after our first skirmish (which is far too embarrassing and trivial to discuss in public), I thought of a simple thing I could do to remind her she is loved: I brought her coffee in bed. Now, for well over thirty years, I have done this morning after morning, through thick and thin, whether we've just had the fight of our lives or are out of town and the coffee shop is five blocks down a rainy street. Unless I'm out of town or she gets up earlier than usual, it's coffee in bed. Sweet of me to do this, right? Of course it is, but I freely confess a Darwinian survival-of-the-fittest motive behind this kindness. Coffee in bed may have prevented a divorce. It virtually guarantees she will wake up about the time other humans do and assures she will be tired enough to turn off her light about the time I'm ready to fall asleep at night. I love the gentle morning light of dawn, but Linda is surprised the few mornings each year she sees the sun rise. Each time, it is for her like the first dawn of a new earth. She is such a late-night person that without coffee at a civilized hour there is no telling whether I would ever sleep. I'm a horrible grump when I'm tired, and the judges and lawyers can tell you it is almost always grumpy people who get divorced. So do you see how coffee in bed saved our marriage? She is so convinced God isn't awake in the morning that for her, it's a waste of time thinking about getting up before he does in case they need to have a talk.

Marriage is never far from the intersection of love and war. What can you do when old wounds reopen, when you have the fight of your life thirty years into your marriage? Linda and I can easily open old wounds and get carried away by our own stupidity. We know exactly where the scars are. It helps when these moments show up to remember we are not the people of our old paradigms. The healing you have experienced is real, even if it is partial. Ground need not be lost because of a fresh episode.

LIGHTEN UP IF YOU WANT TO LIVE

The problem with married people is we take ourselves too seriously, way too seriously. We marry the most perfect creatures we can and then invest our time and energy making them more perfect to fit the image we want or think we deserve. We waste our time criticizing imperfections that don't fit the image we have created for them, or together we create the perfect image of the marriage we want and are surprised when life doesn't cooperate and we can't live up to our own ideals. Perhaps the massive failure of American marriages is connected to such distortions of ourselves.

What makes people act in unloving ways toward those they once loved the most? Does a marriage license also provide a legal right to mistreat those closest to us, to treat each other and our children worse than any other person we know, or to micromanage changes only God is qualified to make? Marriage, to survive the satisfying yet challenging thing it is, must be playful and kind, or it cannot be healthy. It cannot remain sacred if it is not healthy, and it will surely not be full of the life you want and need if it does not remain playful. The light-hearted side of life, the part that gives us balance and makes us happy, like the children we are meant to become, must infuse our attitudes, our emotions, and our deepest life struggles. We have the power to destroy those we love. The trick is not to. In other words, quit acting like everything you say is a revelation from God.

Learn to appreciate the positive power of opposites and how beautiful your differences can be. This power, first and foremost, is love. By it we can create a life worth celebrating, and when we do, the joy of our hearts will provide for others a glimpse now and then of what heaven must be. Marriage is also mystery, and it is part of a larger mystery. Union emotionally, spiritually, physically, and intellectually with a soul who is a polar opposite is a reflection of the mysterious differences and unity we experience with God. In our failings, the differences between us are a wide chasm, yet with love these same differences become the source of great celebration and fulfillment in life. To betray the joyful fountain that sustains you is to destroy part of yourself.

In our failings, the differences between us are a wide chasm, yet with love these same differences become the source of great celebration and fulfillment in life.

What gives marriage its color, spice, and verve? Well, of course, the answer is cherishing people, viewing the world with curiosity, and keeping our eyes open to the differences that enrich us. Not only that, it means accepting life as it comes and caring for each other with the same dignity and respect we want to receive. It is popular to say men want respect more than they want love, and women want love more than they want respect, and perhaps they do, but that seems about as satisfying as having a juicy tomato sandwich minus the tomato or the bread. I am convinced we all want both, and we should. You and those you love are the main characters in the story of your life. Whether yours is a story worth telling depends on how you live it, on how well you love each other.

HOW TO FIGHT A WOMAN'S LOGIC

My wife is an amazing chef and says she can't cook without a TV in the kitchen — and that's not a proposition I want to test. So when one of our brilliant government agencies decreed all television stations were required to begin all-digital broadcasting, the old noise boxes became obsolete overnight. I would have been fine with the static but was ordered by the chef to get a new TV or cook for myself. After I did, the next morning something wasn't working. She asked me to put it back in the box so she could exchange it for another. But the TV would not fit in the box it came in because Chinese people packaged it, and they are smarter than we are. Linda said she would not return it unless the top of the box closed properly. I gave her one of my dirty looks and said something powerful and assertive like, "Sure you will; no one cares whether the box closes or not." She eventually saw my point and agreed to do it.

"Why don't you take the camera battery charger back at the same time and ask them whether it is still under warranty?" I asked.

"No," she said, "I'm not taking back two things. I'd be too embarrassed."

"You expect me to drive twenty miles to Best Buy just to return the battery charger when you're going to be right there, and all you have to do is ask them a question?" I was incredulous but laughing. She was still in bed, sipping the latte I made for her.

"Get out and leave me alone," she growled.

I bowed politely as I backed out of the room and left for work. Like I said, she's not much of a morning person.

Later in the day, she called to say she found a TV she liked better. "Did you return the battery charger?" I asked.

"No," she said, "I'm working on being consistent, and I can't return a TV and the charger and be consistent." she said.

"Consistent with what?" I asked.

"Consistent with myself," she said, "and with my new goal to be consistent."

I thought for a moment and asked her if she was still smelling that smoky, burning smell around her computer and suggested she could pick up some ink while she was out so she could print the first six months of our accounting, just in case of a crash.

"Shoot," she said, "I'll have to go back to Best Buy to get it."

"Why don't you exchange the battery charger while you're there?" I asked. She hung up the phone.

An hour later, she called back steaming. "That's why I don't do exchanges," she said.

"Why is that?" I asked.

"Because somebody from church might be the idiot behind the counter, and I might cuss them out!" she said.

I howled. Who has a wife who comes up with this stuff?

"They said it was still under warranty but refused to replace the charger because I didn't have the camera with me." She was on a roll. "And then when I was all mad because they put conditions no one knows about on honoring the warranty, I ran into our pastor's wife on the way out the door and had to smile and pretend to be nice!"

This is a story from the most mundane part of our life together, but one we will laugh about for a very long time. We'll forget about it, and then one day another stupid thing will happen, or someone will ask a question that will remind us of this little vignette. We'll be sitting around our dinner table laughing again at our idiocy, at our own lives and the odd way we live them, and we will be thankful for the love that is the running theme in all our stories, even those we almost ruined when we were angry.

Some of the craziest and most frustrating episodes of life make the best stories. Later, that is. Like the cheap hotel in Knoxville. (Don't ask.) Or my son's head injury that kept him talking in a loop for two anxious hours. Or the loony aunt whose underwear fell off in the middle of the Nashville airport. *Please* don't ask. Or the folks who called begging to stay with us at 2:00 a.m. because the Mormons were after them. We didn't know until then it is possible to go straight from a dead sleep to a belly laugh. Or the relative who stole the wedding wine and pickles from our daughter's wedding. Or the first time Linda tried to crack open a lobster tail and it flipped out of her hand and landed on the plate of a sophisticated lady in Bar Harbor. We were crying we were laughing so hard. Some stories are meant to be continued for our blessing years after they begin, like the flower delivery lady who showed up to thank us for inviting their family in for dinner when her husband knocked on our door twenty years earlier to sell insurance. After dinner that evening, I gave him a Bible and suggested it could make a difference in his life if he read it. A simple kindness, his wife told us, changed his life and theirs.

Our life stories are at least partially sacred — even the crazy ones, the silly ones, the sorrowful ones. *Especially* the sorrowful ones! Don't ruin or erase the stories of your life because of anger or embarrassment or disagreements or infidelity. Create them, collect them, celebrate them, tell them again and again to your children, and enjoy the new ones day in and day out as they happen. And don't leave out the broken stories. They become more valuable as time goes by.

Mom used to smile about some of the things that energized feminists and how the movement reflected, as much as anything, the image women held of themselves. She prayed constantly for them to discover even higher purposes. She believed women should be paid fairly, well respected, and free to accomplish anything they wanted to accomplish. She did not believe in glass ceilings, and she wasn't concerned that feminists were expecting too much but rather that they were expecting too little. Why be like men, she mused, when you can actually be a woman? Why settle for equality with men? If you knew Mom, there wasn't one bone of superiority in her, so this wasn't about elevation over men either.

What *was* it all about, I wanted to know? She told me her role model was Mary, the mother of Jesus, who was blessed above all women and was visited by angels sent from God who addressed her with supreme dignity. Her prayer for feminists, she said, was that women would come to know, as she had, how richly blessed and respected they are by God because they are women. Once they know that, she said, no man, no society, no religion, no traditions or customs, no regulations or restrictions, no inequities, *nothing* can take away the glory of being a woman. With this attitude came an unshakable confidence about life, about relationships, and about herself. Her identity was connected to her husband, but it was not derived from him. The gentle dignity and strength of womanhood, she knew, did not require it.

THE POWER TO CREATE LIFE OR DESTROY IT

What does this have to do with men and the power of opposites? Plenty. Perhaps the most damaging predispositions among men in relationship with their families are domination and control, precisely what feminists and men of character reject as an acceptable standard. But men are not alone in this weakness. Women who try to shape their sons into the husbands and fathers they *wish* they had, or who try by excessive control to prevent sons from becoming like the men in their lives who hurt them, also need a new way of thinking. When a young man reaches adolescence, a mother needs a deep understanding of the damage that extreme control does in the boy now reaching manhood. A healthy father can help her understand this, but few men understand how to communicate these delicate issues with gentleness, strength, and wisdom. This time of radical change in a young man needs to be counterbalanced by wise parents united enough to guide him and to increasingly allow him to experience the results of his own choices so he can discover the roots and limits of his own existence and manhood. Healthy balance between parents at this time in a son's life is one of the most difficult things to achieve. Divorced parents who insist on making their children their personal battleground have even more at risk.

Men, I think, have an intrinsic fear of the power they have to destroy themselves. Perhaps women do too. We know how to start wars, but we don't really know much about stopping them and healing the wounds of our warfare. Somehow the brilliance of two vastly different creatures, needing each other not only to survive but to live, seems more than a sinister evolutionary blunder. Together we cocreate life, not only in procreation, but in twenty-four-hour segments filled with celebrations, the weary mundane, sorrows enough to silence hell, and joy sometimes to give us the wings of heaven. Whatever beauty we created or destroyed yesterday, we will have a fresh start the moment the sun rises (provided, at our house, there is coffee in bed). What we do together when it does, one little day at a time, determines everything.

We are attracted initially because of what we have in common, yet also by the mystery we discover in each other. We call this finding our soul mate. I've never heard anyone say the reason they got married is because they had little to nothing in common with their spouse, but the longer you live, the more you know it is the distinctions, not the similarities, between men and women that make life worth living. They are the sparkle that keeps a good marriage going.

Three young women came to dinner one night and wanted to know how we managed to stay married for so long. Then they asked us what our fights are like. We laughed and gave them a few examples of our temporary insanity, our own homemade sin. Most of what worries us in the moment does not make a hill of beans' worth of difference, we said, but it is often the little things that ambush us. Any couple, we told them, could find some reason for a divorce without looking very far. Not a *sufficient* reason, but enough to throw in the towel, if only because life is hard. Linda and I made a promise after we married never to bring up "the D word." We would always work to find our way through whatever difficulties come along. She has promised not to divorce me, even if I were ever unfaithful to her. First-degree murder, without a doubt, but not divorce.

So guys, resolve to walk with integrity of heart within your house, the place you are most likely to make your first compromise. Create a healthy relationship with your wife. Be not less than a best friend to her, but more. Keep your life playful, not treating your wife as a sex object, yet enjoying your shared sexuality to the fullest. Give her the love, respect, and dignity you want for yourself, acknowledging that the two of you are equals in an enterprise God wants to honor and bless. Celebrate her strength and the vast differences that make her a woman and you a man. Do not mar her beauty. Be gentle with her weakness, and pray that God will give you confidence to be the man she needs. Help her find her distinctive voice—a voice that for you will be like the balm of Gilead rather than the sorrowful voice of Eve the day the angels sent our first parents away from the garden where they had once walked and talked with God as two unique and separate individuals, united with each other in complete intimacy.

SEVEN

WHERE THE BEAUTY STARTS

MEN HAVE A GOD-GIVEN APPETITE FOR beauty and an equally deep and native yearning to achieve and enjoy the honor and dignity we observe in men we respect. These two attributes — beauty and honor — are the two most powerful driving forces in men. They are stronger than sex, stronger than our competitive edge, stronger than our fears, and perhaps even stronger than our instincts for survival. By them, civilizations are formed and prosper. In fact, they are the tools we use to survive.

Men are attracted to beauty. In addition to the most obvious attraction of men (watch his eyes — you'll see), men are attracted to great architecture, to the natural beauty of a canyon or mountain wilderness, to the beauty of a sunset, to the symmetry of a flock of birds or a school of fish, to the incomprehensible vastness of the universe. We love the sleek lines of a Porsche, the classic style of a rusted Ford pickup, the beauty of an old slate roof, and the innocent eyes of a child. We can be moved by art, by patterns in a snowflake, by the exquisite colors and designs in nature. We are in awe of every micro- and macro-frontier known to man, to old beauty and to new, and to the unfathomable beauty of the love of God, once we find it.

Our deepest attraction is to love. All other attractions and appetites are expressions of our desire for love. Whether this attribute in a man is marred or completely obscured by sorrows or years of abuse, whether he can say it aloud or admit it to himself, who he is at his core is a man in search of love. His addictions and perversions are mere proof of his desire gone wild.

As it is with the pursuit of beauty, as long as men have existed, they have devoted their lives to the pursuit of honor. Perhaps it is the result of Eden. Perhaps it is because we are created in the image of God. Or both. Men give their lives in sacrifice for their children, their wives, their beliefs, their friends, and their countries. In service to honor, men fight wars and pay an untold price to preserve for others the blessings of freedom. They throw their bodies over grenades on the front lines of battle to save their friends. They face dangers of all kinds to save a child, and as the entire world saw with its own eyes on 9/11, they will climb towering infernos to save the lives of people they do not know.

> **Men have a God-given appetite for beauty and an equally deep and native yearning to achieve and enjoy the honor and dignity we observe in men we respect. These two attributes — beauty and honor — are the two most powerful driving forces in men.**

In honor of truth, men tied to burning stakes have died rather than deny their faith in Jesus Christ. The story is told in the history of the martyrs of the church of Dirk Willems, who turned to rescue the man pursuing him from the icy water into which he had fallen, only to be arrested by that same man and killed for his faith. The fact that honor could offer such a scene is proof that deep in the heart of a man transformed by the presence of Jesus Christ is a pure strain of gold, a dignity conferred on him by the Master, attributes in a man whose story is told for generations to come.

Beauty and honor are the two most basic and dynamic architectural elements of a man's soul. When he is young, a boy is drawn first and quickly toward beauty, but he must be taught honor. In a healthy family where his father cherishes his mother, the young lad first encounters beauty in his mother. His mother's respect for his father confers to him his first encounter with honor. When he is older and has learned that life is not worth living without honor, he must have both honor and beauty, and they must be in balance, one revealing the other, each giving the other its elegant grace, like the dance of two lovers enthralled in each other's arms.

Some men spend their lives in pursuit of what, exactly, they do not know—the money, the retirement dream, beautiful women, the image of superiority to their brothers, the mountains left to conquer, or the things that might have been but are not. Others, who discover early enough that they must have a purpose greater than their egos, dedicate their lives to humanity or to God, or in humility to God *and* to humanity. This is good, but under it all, both those in self-absorbed pursuit and men with the noblest motives have the quest of beauty and honor as their internal fuel cell. In one, the motive and the quest are marred; in the other, less so.

Beauty and honor must be alive together, or both will die. The raw pursuit of beauty alone need not, but can, lead a man to pornography. The pursuit of honor for honor's sake need not, but can, lead him toward abuse or legalism or unnecessary harshness. Righteousness and peace kissing each other are a life-giving pair, and in our equation, it is gentleness and strength of beauty and honor woven together that yields the desirable sum. A man's fascination with beauty may cause him to look long at a woman's body. It is honor that causes him to look into her eyes, where he finds the beauty of her soul.

> **A man must have both honor and beauty, and they must be in balance, one revealing the other, each giving the other its elegant grace, like the dance of two lovers enthralled in each other's arms.**

Why did God create men with such an intense desire for beauty and with an equally strong desire for respect and honor? It is because of the goodness of God that man is so created. We were created for and destined to a world in which we will gaze on pure beauty, where perfect passion — so rare it is reserved for the pure in heart — will see the beauty of God. We will gaze on a beauty that is the absolute, radiant glory of God. Such beauty, such glory, would waste us were we to see it now, and so we are impaired as those who "see through a glass, darkly."[1] Yet in Christ, we beheld his glory, glory as of the only begotten of the Father, and what we shall soon see, recognized first in Christ, remains for us, for now, unspeakable.[2] Take hope in this, good brothers.

With David, the great king and songwriter of Israel, we pray, "One thing have I asked of the LORD ...: that I may dwell in the house of the LORD ..., *to gaze upon the beauty of the LORD and to inquire in his temple*."[3] If you could ask but one thing of the Lord, would it be to gaze on his beauty? What beauty are we missing when we look at God? When we do not look at God? What have we not yet seen that David longed for so dearly? What is our inheritance, about which we know so very little? We will be future observers of beauty we cannot

A man's fascination with beauty may cause him to look long at a woman's body. It is honor that causes him to look into her eyes, where he finds the beauty of her soul.

even imagine today. If that were not enough, we will have conferred on us the eternal dignities and respect reserved for those who are members of the royal family of God. This is the reason we long so dearly for honor and respect as men. God plans to grant to us this rarely spoken desire imprinted so deep in our hearts we can barely mumble the reality of it. We seldom speak of it, but we know.

HOPE FOR VISUAL LEARNERS

Those of us who knew the modern-day Southern saint Bob Benson smile when we remember things he said and did. One thing he always did the best he could was to be honest. When a beautiful woman walked past, on more than one occasion, Bob, rather than pretend he did not see her or that she did not exist, simply said, "Isn't God good?" And so he is.

The big joke about men looking at women is that we are visual learners, and so we can't help ourselves. To some degree, we can't. It is normal to look, but it is the man who looks in lust who commits the sin. My wife has been helpful throughout our marriage. Rather than ignore the obvious, she has often commented on another woman's beauty or said, "Isn't she pretty?" helping me admit out loud what we both already knew, thereby making no big deal about it for me or between us. She does not appreciate it, of course, if I keep looking, so I try not to.

When it comes to beauty, men *are* visual learners, but we are much more. We desire mystery, the honor of worthy conquest, romance, friendship, meaningful conversation, a worthwhile life purpose and work, and, ultimately, we desire heaven. It is sad to see so many men give up on their dreams and even sadder to see them set the course of their lives on dreams that have no more value than the dust of the grave.

God is calling the men of this and every generation to rise up from the dust and death of their own vices to be "oaks of righteousness," men in whom he will create beauty to replace the ashes of a burned-out life.[4] He is calling young men in their strength to devote themselves to the majestic vision of following in the footsteps of Jesus Christ. He is calling older men to live life to the fullest, to produce fruit as a green tree with leaves that do not wither, even in old age, and as fathers to lead their younger brothers in the wisdom they have learned through many years of following Jesus. God wants a deep community of faith engaged in the conversations and fellowship of brotherly love, intent on one purpose, united in spirit, and leading their homes, their businesses, and their communities to do what is right and good. He wants to awaken sleeping men, as the apostle Paul writes in his letter to believers in Ephesus, and to raise them from the dead so that Christ will shine on them.[5]

HOME IS WHERE THE BEAUTY STARTS

It is not common to think of men as homemakers. Nor does the sound of it, in the context of women and stereotypes, resonate well in most social circles. But the idea of making home the center, the place where honor and beauty meet and create life, is worth more than a glance. In such an extraordinary world, a man has as much to do with the kind of home he lives in as a woman does. He does this without the loss of dignity; in fact, it is an authentic source of dignity for him. He finds his place with grace and strength and bows to serve, whether or not anyone else does. Guys who think this has something to do with controlling the color of the soup bowls in the cupboard need to be recircumcised. What it does mean is that healthy men have as much to do with the life-giving environment of the home as their wives. Children living in such homes know the supreme consequences of love. The fountainhead of the pleasant streams of life begins in loving families, where both parents contribute everything they are to make a house a home. In so doing, they are transformed from what they were to a new unified creation, itself an image of what they will yet become in the perfect kingdom of God.

> **Healthy men have as much to do with the life-giving environment of the home as their wives.**

It's easy for a man to check out, say nothing, do nothing, be nothing, or to be so heavy-handed he becomes a domestic dictator. Both extremes are born of insecurities or apathy. Nothing "fouls the nest" like apathy. Nothing is more miserable for families than men who downgrade themselves into control freaks. Neither extreme taps the life-giving well of fatherhood or honors a mother's heart and passion for the welfare of her family. To be and know something less than what is true is to be very little.

Homes where beauty and honor reside in peace are carefree, light-hearted, and good. This does not mean they are without struggles, that they are perfect or wonderful at every moment of every day. But they are safe for adults and for children, and they are good. This goodness is bountiful, beautiful, and kind and is an invitation to become creatures of love we could not have become if left to ourselves.

Despite every contrary evolutionary theory, men love the kind of beauty that flows from a healthy home. They want it as much as women do, sometimes more. Two days after Eliot Spitzer resigned as governor of New York, one psychologist on a network morning show theorized that cavorting with multiple sex partners "like the polygamous animal kingdom" was normal in our evolutional development. We should not, this psychologist was sure, consider ourselves above pure animal behavior. That Spitzer had the ability to reason, wrongly, was no evidence to him of a superior human ethic or intellect. What the governor lost in just one news cycle was the reality he needed and wanted most in life. That his behavior over several years proved he was looking in all the wrong places does not destroy my thesis that what he desired most was waiting for him at home. Somehow, sadly, he set aside honor and beauty for trifles, for glitter and gold dust that vanish in the light.

> **Homes where beauty and honor reside in peace are carefree, lighthearted, and good.**

When a man loses what he knew as the warmth and welcome of home, the loving embrace of his wife, the cheerful voices of his children, the laughter and sounds of celebration and joy he knows in the presence of his friends, the welcome he receives because he is Dad, it is then he knows that the most important beauty that attracts men is the beauty of home. If he did not discern it before, at the moment it is lost he knows it is *this beauty* in which a man finds supreme satisfaction and joy. Beauty at home in the mundane and ordinary routines is the fountain of all good flowing from a man's life. It is a temporary, magnificent deception to think otherwise.

Sin creates loneliness. Do not take me to mean that loneliness is sin or that all loneliness is the result of sin. But mark this, and mark it well: Sin does create isolation, separation, segregation, and self-delusion on the order of legal blindness. What happens to a man when he has so lost his way is entirely predictable, but most men who try to live by their own standards think they can beat the odds. Few, if any, ever do.

Home should be a sacred place, a place where tears are safe, a place of trust, of joy and celebration, a place where common bread and wine are holy.

In one of our "Dinner and Conversation" discussions, I asked the brothers to describe what they want their homes to be in the next twenty years. There's a question you seldom hear men answer. We talked about it for several hours. The memorable answer, for me, came from my friend Gary. He said he wanted his home to be a place where his grandchildren always wanted to come, where they were excited to see Papa. Then he said, "And I also want my home to be more like church, or more like what church is supposed to be." What he meant is that home should be a sacred place, a place where tears are safe, a place of trust, of joy and celebration, a place where common bread and wine are holy.

Home should be a place where children are safe, where God sits down at our table because he enjoys our presence and we enjoy his. That's not far-fetched, if you believe the words of Jesus: "Behold, I stand at the door and knock. If anyone hears my voice and opens the door, I will come in to him and eat with him, and he with me."[6]

I can tell you this. God came to our house. He came right in our front door and sat down at our table and ate with us. Did we see him?

Well, no, not at first, but we did recognize his presence. We did see his royal beauty and the noble honor he brought to our house. He brought us laughter and gifts of joy we did not have, and he brought us some of the tears he cries, so we now can cry them too. Before he came, we did not know that he cries, or why. But now we know. We've had many friends tell us they find these qualities in our home, and we know they were not there before *he* came to dinner. So it must be true, because our friends are not liars, and we did not tell them to say this about the place we now call home.

The next time he knocks at your door, invite him in. He's not a picky eater. Tell him you know us, and if you want to see beauty and honor up close and personal, give him a chance. He's quite something, really. I hope he stops by soon.

EIGHT

SORROW — THE HAND THAT SHAPES US

IN THE DAYS WHEN HOBOS WALKED long country roads looking for a friendly farmhouse and a back step off the kitchen porch where they could sit down to a warm meal and a kind word, Momma never sent them away. In my first memory of these strangers, I hid and watched under the kitchen table until the man ate and walked on down the road. Momma told me not to be afraid — he was a nice man, very polite, just hungry. At three years old, I did not know what *hungry* was or understand that *love* is the verb that makes the Christian faith so practical. She told me these strangers could be angels sent from God to bless us. Who knows? Perhaps they were.

Our home was constantly filled with hungry people, and Mom and Dad always fed and talked with them. It was one of their irresistible expressions of Christian love. Over the years, literally thousands of people from around the world sat at the table of my parents, humble and quiet country people with a little food and a great deal of love. Ambassadors from Pakistan and Africa, farm aid officials from Washington, homeless people, neighbors in a whale of trouble, funny tourists from New York and Boston, missionaries from Costa Rica, a Palestinian student born in Bethlehem who was probably some relative of Joseph the carpenter, kids up the street whose parents decided to divide their lives into fragments, a troubled aunt who lived with us, Amish and Mennonite relatives by the dozen, and foster kids who had grown up and didn't even know their parents. I can't remember a supper that wasn't followed by a song or a few lines of verse the entire family would recite together.

My parents' guest books that span five decades record the story, the names of those who shared their lives with us in a moment of time. The first entry records a visitor from Ethiopia, the third from the Netherlands. How they came to eat at our table I do not know, but from my earliest memory I understood that the world is a global neighborhood with a common need for love, community, understanding, kindness, and celebration. Dad, a brilliant man with only an eighth-grade education, welcomed people of every stripe and color into our home, and he loved to learn something new from each of them.

That every person has intrinsic value because God loves them was the lesson I learned at my parents' table. Neither their high positions nor their broken-down life circumstances ever changed the way Mom and Dad loved them all. The single-lane dirt road intersection dividing our farm, used for horse-drawn buggies and farm implements, pointed to villages and cities around the world. Our table, in a small way, was the center of the world, the heart of our existence.

SONS OF SORROW

Perhaps I was crazy, addled by a kind of self-inflicted spiritual mad cow disease (we were dairy farmers, after all), but I once asked God to permit me to enter the sorrows of my brothers to better understand them and to help me become present with men in their pain and sorrow. I do not remember whether the impetus came from a brush with one of the Desert Fathers on a dreamy moonlit night, the idea that Jesus wants to show us something about love through excruciating pain, my unwillingness to live a shallow life, or all of the above. It was probably my iteration of what I saw Dad and Mom doing all their lives, or at least the result of one of those many whispered prayers Mom lifted up for a young and arrogant son. Whatever I was thinking, I requested not only wisdom but insight as well, and something more to offer than "I am sorry" when the world falls apart in the lives of men around me. It must have been a prayer "according to his will," the "kind of prayer he hears," because all hell broke loose—to the point I have begun to wonder whether all prayers he hears have the power to break hell.

Whether saying such things to God is a smart thing to do remains in doubt for those who are afraid of him. What I began to experience, however, was life at a deeper level than I had known. To see in the eyes and faces of friends and others the unspeakable sorrows of their souls, to hear in a new way the stories of their bereavement and suffering, is to become more human. In these sons of sorrow I found brothers who had never spoken a word about their insecurities, abuse, failures, or anger, but who in the presence of a friend were willing to speak them out loud for the first time in their lives. I discovered how difficult it is for men to express deep joy or for their souls to unite with beauty and truth. And as we talked, I began to experience my own sorrows and became more aware of my inadequacy to love and receive love or to believe I am always loved by our Father no matter what. My perfect view of myself, which I loved so much, began to crack until it left me standing naked in the presence of God.

This is what happens when one is "married to Truth," though standing naked in the presence of God is not a concept I was well taught or one I learned until I became unafraid to permit him to help me examine my own imperfections. I first heard of naked honesty in an atmosphere of guilt and shame, and I was afraid of this bizarre idea, afraid just as Adam must have been in Eden, meeting God without his pants in his first spiritual postmortem after the fall. How *does* a very dead man meet a very alive God? Most of us parade behind our party masks or work harder to make the trains run on time, hoping God will pick the guy next to us and allow us to slide by unnoticed until we can get our act together. But when a man is uncovered before God with nothing to hide, and he realizes he is safe in God's presence, it provides the sense for the first time in his life that he is actually fully clothed in the presence of others, that he can be accepted for who he really is.

There are losses and sorrows for which there are no words, deep groans that have no language. I have never heard of any man making it to the end of his life without them. Few men comprehend this while they are young, and I knew no one in my youth who intentionally prepared himself for this season of life. I did not understand the connection between sorrow and reality. Our unspeakable sorrows frequently arrive through death or in difficult or disfigured relationships with children, parents, spouses, or friends. They come to us precisely through those relational tributaries designed by God to give life, but where refreshing streams of living water should flow there is instead the overwhelming stench of stagnant swamp water sent by some clever but moronic demon to drown us. And when sorrow and difficulties seem too sad, too painful, and unending, how on earth, we want to know, will God be able to take this mess and make it one of his "all things" that "work together for good"?[1]

> When a man is uncovered before God with nothing to hide, and he realizes he is safe in God's presence, it provides the sense for the first time that he is actually fully clothed in the presence of others, that he can be accepted for who he really is.

Perhaps what follows will help you, as it has helped me, not only to believe but to understand and to see. Not only to see, but to trust. Not only to trust, but to cling to hope as we are comforted and assured, because hope does not disappoint.

THE VALUE OF TROUBLE

The blues is some of the most beautiful music in the world. Plaintive, lost, honest, painful, and hard-earned licks and riffs celebrate the sorrows and little delights of life. A kiss from my baby. A warm cup of coffee. The bell at the end of a long, hot day. You can't be a much-too-young American idol and sing the blues, which is why I get along just fine with Mississippi John, one of my favorite American hardscrabble musicians. Mississippi John's music was never popular until after he died, and it was only a fluke that any of it was recorded at all—one old man sitting on his rocker on a beat-up porch, house falling down around his ears, singing and playing the songs of his soul.

Without the blues carried down the street on the gentle evening breeze at the end of another hard day, in desperate times you might as well roll over and die. Your soul knows you must sing if you are to live. *Listen.* It is the song of your sorrows, yet it is also a song of joy. It is the song that celebrates your life. It is a dirge and a dance. It is the music of your Creator and your song woven together, written in your heart—a melody deep within you that no one but you can sing. Some men never sing their song. Some sing only the songs of others, and some never sing at all.

Ask others to tell you the most difficult circumstances of their lives, and you will find the stories breathtaking, woven in weakness, failure, sorrow, and grief. The weary survivors seldom know how they made it through, how they lived in the storms of destruction, how they found life after the deforming processes of sorrow reshaped them. A word or the touch of a friend sustained them. Someone or something provided a spark of hope so little it was almost invisible—one spark of hope stuck somewhere in the crevasse of a broken heart that could not be dislodged by darkness, by despair, or by devils of the black night.

What have they learned from their hardships? I want to know. Has the value of what they discovered surpassed the cost of their sorrows? Some do not know, but no one ever says they want to repeat the experiences. The overwhelming majority I have asked, however, say they do not want to lose what they gained though difficult experiences.

In this way, true spirituality can be counterintuitive. One summer evening in our neighborhood, one dear family held a wake for their twenty-one-year-old son, whose tragic death made no sense, while two doors down, a house full of happy women celebrated a young bride about to be married. If "it is better to go to the house of mourning than to go to the house of feasting," as Solomon wrote, what are we to learn from sorrow?[2] What will she say to us while she twists and breaks us, shatters to little pieces what we thought was, until then, a reasonable and good life? What does sadness from divorce, suicide, cancer, financial ruin, death, and estrangement want to teach us? Is sorrow a kind of protection from something worse? Sadness, an early warning system? Grief, the doorway to an otherwise elusive peace, the hidden entrance to something better? There are no easy answers.

To keep our pain from becoming so debilitating, we do almost anything to avoid the full weight of our suffering. We medicate, withdraw, create elaborate lies, become emotional abusers, and invent plausible denials to manage our mess. Soon these manipulations can take on a life of their own. Of this I am entirely sure.

Such raw emotional pain in others freaks out rule keepers who have not yet become honest about their own pain. In fact, one stream of pietistic religion identifies any show of raw feeling in the face of emotional pain as sin. The Bible will have none of it. Nor do the Scriptures condemn screaming in the midst of physical pain. I have known half-people all my life, and so have you. Their trade is religious superiority and cloaked abuse. They play the common parlor game of pride and talk of humility before they have learned it. They ride above the average guy and cannot stoop or kneel to feel the crucifying pain of others. These are the ones who say, "I'm fine," when almost nothing is truly fine. Beware the fixers and religious police who wear crosses as emblems and bear Holy Scriptures as weapons against their brothers and do not yet know *they* must be borne on their own crosses. Make sure you are not one of them, for there is no way to escape the ultimate paradox of life.

Reaction to pain and sorrow can be involuntary, like a sneeze or a scream. Children cooperate quickly with pain. Grown-ups — if there are such things—do not cooperate so quickly. Our reactions to pain are more calculated. Song-killing sorrow left to wander in the wild places of the heart, we fear, will become a demon of immense proportion and power whose only song is a screeching howl in the night. We are afraid of *that* song, of our own howls and cries and of the sorrowful groans and screams of others. We crush the dynamic range of the melody being written in our lives so we do not have to face our own demented image or hear our own broken melodies, the laments we must sing before our voices will ever blend in the beautiful song of the Great Dance.

The Man of Sorrows wants to live with us in the full dynamic range of our sorrow. In fact, he became incarnate among us to set us free, not to help us deny we are here. The wide dynamic of honesty and truth is the only place where there is room for the fully formed Christ to exist. Otherwise he must stand aside, outside our pain. While he may comfort, in part, with a kind hand on our shoulder, he cannot live within the center of our painful existence until we are ready to confess the full experience of life.

Weaker than we knew, we have allowed our sorrows to describe us. As men, our silence confines us; our weariness immobilizes us. Because our sorrows have overwhelmed us, we become easy prey. Joy, our strength and our protection, has gone down the chute. We must, therefore, learn to invite Jesus into our pain, our suffering, and our sorrows, as he invites us into his. He is connected to our pain, and our pain is connected to him. He becomes present, incarnate, Immanuel, God with us in our howls and our screams; we become present in his cries, his prayers, his tears, and his loneliness in Gethsemane, the place on earth that most nearly embodies the torment of every broken heart. He wants us to desire the fellowship of his suffering because we are already present *in* his suffering. In this suffering we locate our individuality, our humanity, and ourselves. It is where we stumble upon "the God of all comfort," where our immortal identity is found, preserved, and fulfilled. Sorrow makes it possible for us to draw near to God when we would draw near to him by no other means. This is the work of a friend.

Author Robert Benson makes a brilliant observation: "Every time I go looking for God, I find myself."* God is the only one who can give you the *true you*. Conformed to his death in sorrow and pain, we are given the resurrection and the life we could not receive in any other way. We should take comfort that he is "a man of sorrows, and acquainted with grief" because so are we.[3] Until we knew better, we hid our faces from him. But when we pray "your will be done," we grant permission to the Holy One to form what we have made unholy into his image yet again and to make us stop treating God like a child or a servant. We are asking him to complete his work. We are respecting his decision with his creation. We are saying that Father knows best. We want him, in this brief moment of our sanity, to override every other insane moment of our lives with our prayer "your will be done." There will be moments when we cannot pray it, moments perhaps when we cannot pray at all. We ask him now to hear this prayer, this petition according to his will, and to ignore and override all other prayers we might ask of him in our pain, suffering, or insanity that may contradict his holy will, now or in the future. This, brothers, is the prayer of a man given to Jesus, unconcerned that his personal good as he sees it may have been compromised, certain and content that God will do with us only what is truly good. This is not theory. This is not myth. This is the living reality of God's loving his family, caring for them, providing in such a way as to ensure that we arrive at the destination for which he has created us. Do we not yet know we cannot do this for ourselves?

In the fellowship of Christ's suffering, we find a truthful friendship, an authentic sorrow, and a dependable comfort. This spiritual friendship may be the closest thing to home we experience in this world, and it is our doorway to joy and peace. This, too, is counterin-

---

* In a conversation with Robert Benson, author of *The Echo Within*.

tuitive, another paradox of the kingdom of God, but once we experience it along with our brothers and are restored, Jesus will never again be an abstraction.

At dinner one evening with a couple of friends, it dawned on me that asking Jesus into my sorrows is as simple as inviting my brothers into my grief, allowing them to share it with me. As I did, these two "priests" I've known for over thirty years spoke into my "confession" like wise, old prophets sent from God. "Do not try to understand this with your intellect," they said. "All you need to do is love this guy who is hurting you. You can't reach him with reason, but he will not be able to resist love." Their voices and laughter sounded something like Jesus. The insights they provided, the peace they brought to my conflict, the instruction they offered for my life, the shelter of their kindness, the

> When we pray "your will be done," we grant permission to the Holy One to form what we have made unholy into his image yet again and to make us stop treating God like a child or a servant.[4] We are asking him to complete his work.

bread and the wine we shared—these gifts became the table of God's presence. Jesus, present in and through these dear brothers, restored my weary soul and reaffirmed the true narrative of my life, the one he is telling through me. The memory of this conversation remains in my mind as the night those sorrows began to dance, where theories about fellowship and suffering and brothers melded into the celebration of friendship and life.

LOVE RESTORES MORE THAN IT TAKES

Sorrow and joy can exist separately but seldom do. Truth and freedom can exist only together. It is the law of God. Take your freedom without truth, and you will soon experience bondage of your will, the will you swore was recently so free and good. You will be the slave of uncooperative delusions that betray the very idea of freedom. Employ truth as a means of binding others, and you will soon find them in a state of revolution. The history of dictators, legalists, and local control freaks argues that something deep within them is afraid of the marriage of truth and freedom, afraid of love. It is the fear that they will lose something they possess, something they have taken illicitly, something to which they have no right. Freedom encourages truth. Truth generates freedom. Truth and freedom destroy illusions. Sorrow and joy provide the song by which we celebrate our freedom and the pleasures of life.

When Jesus declares himself to be the way, the truth, and the life, he stands against all lies, all manipulation, all death, all plots and schemes, all deceit, and all religious spirits.[5] He will destroy every evil stronghold. As the exact representation of his Father, nothing is his rival or his equal. No plan of his can be thwarted. Nothing can get around him, for he blocks the path. He is the door, and beyond him is life, and he requires all who enter life to bow down in repentance before him. No one who has ever bowed in humility and sorrow has been turned away. Before each man stands a cross — the naked, sacred cross of Christ — and we must encounter his cross if we are to meet him.

Take your freedom without truth, and you will soon experience bondage of your will, the will you swore was recently so free and good.

The place of the cross for him and for us is a place of enormous sorrow. At this place, he gave up his life, his greatness, and the presence of his Father. On this cross, he made himself empty, giving up each and every right for us. When we come to the cross, we do the same. We give up our reputation, our own way, our rebellion, our masks, our false self, and the little bit of greatness we have collected. Above all, we give up our distorted wills so they can be replaced with something new.

Until we do, we cannot know how great and satisfying the exchange will be. The cross becomes our legal writ for joy. Love always replaces more than it takes, and the pure love of the Father requires us to give our most precious holdings so he can give us our lavish inheritance. First and foremost, our inheritance is the presence of the resurrected Jesus in our day-to-day existence, but next—and just as important, because we cannot be separated from his goodness—is the blessing of brothers, men who have received their inheritance and have been set free. This is what makes the Christian faith practical, celebratory, and true. All other blessings flow to us and through us because Jesus is alive, loving us here and now.

DAILY BREAD FOR DAILY SORROWS

How many men do you know who are full of joy? Can you name even one? Jesus said he came so that his joy may be in us and that our joy may be full, but when I look around our communities and our churches, joy is not what comes to mind.[6] That's just one reason I talk so much about celebration, about bringing daily bread into our daily routines and making of it a feast and a delight. After knowing without a doubt that we are loved by God, the greatest need men have right now is for more joy, but our fears and our sorrows have undone us. I'm tired of the Christian mantra that says, "God is more interested in our joy than in our happiness," which has become nothing more than an apology for why followers of Jesus are so grouchy and hard to please. We have even made spirituality sad, as though we were in divorce proceedings with God. Poets and songwriters know it is easier to write something sad and dark than to create beauty filled with joy. Perhaps it is because our sorrows seem so concrete, so tangible, and ever present, while joy remains so elusive. Men, I think, are more likely to get stuck in their sorrows than to walk beyond "the valley of the shadow."

When I was in my midtwenties, I lost my way, as only a young man can who finds himself in a strange city with few friends and loneliness to spare. One morning after a sad and unfulfilling night in the arms of a one-night stand, I was driving to work with tears coursing down my face. I could barely see the road, and I was desperate and pleading with God to help me. The very moment I called for help, a beautiful bluebird flew into the windshield of my car and dropped dead onto the road. Bluebirds have always been my favorites, my little friends in the bird kingdom. I'm too color-blind to see half the cardinals in the woods, but the vibrant colors of the bluebird have always caught my eye. When I cried out to God that morning and my beautiful little friend flew into my car a split second later, I wailed, "God, why? Why did that little innocent bird have to die?" In that moment I heard this thought, *Every time you sin, something beautiful dies and sings no more.*

> After knowing without a doubt that we are loved by God, the greatest need men have right now is for more joy, but our fears and our sorrows have undone us.

If this is true, the stunning thing to me is how much death and dying happen while a man learns to live, yet how the spark of resurrection can make him alive again, no matter the circumstances. My father often told me there were dead men walking around, guys who had lost their hearts, who gave them one little bit at a time to the things that kill men. It is easy to see this in what we consider to be the big moral failures, but it is just as true with the "little junk" we embrace as normal parts of our character or personality. Whether you give your life away "one little brick at a time" or in a moment of great moral failure, the song of your heart is dying, slowly dying. Your heart will kill you, unless there is some remedy.

At Mom's funeral, her pastor asked the nearly five hundred guests how many of them had ever been to my parents' home for a meal. Our family turned around to view a sea of hands, and while there must have been a few, we could not see anyone whose hand was not raised. Their table, for fifty-five years, welcomed all who came.

Likewise, the table of our Lord represents restoration and a warm welcome home into his presence with fellow sinners when the songbird of your life has fallen dead on the side of the road. Enemies, including those we have created, come to steal, to kill, and to destroy us, but Jesus offers his broken body and his blood as divine restoration from our foes in what we now celebrate and receive in the Holy Eucharist as daily bread for daily sorrows. The fact that wine and bread, the symbols of *joy* and of *life* in which are locked away the sacred mysteries of God, should be endowed with such significance is a reality only God could conceive. We receive the holy remedy, the sacred mystery. We offer it to one another. We receive Jesus again and again and are given the right to become the children of God. "Do this in remembrance of me," Jesus said, for in his presence, there is fullness of joy. Perhaps the table at your house could become, if it is not already, the table of the presence of the Lord, not only for yourself and your family, but also for others.

For those who are dying or have already died because of their own sin and sorrow—or at the point of their enemy's sword—Jesus invites you to receive him. In this way, he turns our sorrow into joy, our mourning into dancing, and destroys in our hearts death, over which we had no power. There is nothing that more clearly reflects the life of Jesus than the light of the world shining through the prism of a man's tears as he

Every time you sin, something beautiful dies and sings no more.

enjoys the feast at the table of our dear Lord. They are the tears that fall freely from the faces of men who have seen the glory of God.

Perhaps it is the duty of sorrow to prepare us for the joys of heaven and to make of us children who may enter the kingdom of God.

NINE

THE TOUGH YEARS

He who would escape the mill that grinds slow and grinds small,
must yield to the hammer and chisel; for those who refuse to be
stones of the living temple must be ground into mortar for it.

George MacDonald, *Castle Warlock*

SOME MEN WANT TO LIVE IN the light. Other men prefer darkness. Others want the half-light, where there is enough darkness to cover their evil intentions and sufficient light to convince others they want to do what is right. These are the dangerous men who infiltrate and pollute our feasts to use brothers for their own gain.[1]

This isn't about what happened to me but about what happened inside me. Please remember that. It is the story of three betrayals and some expensive yet life-saving lessons.

Several years ago, I was completely surprised by how uncooperative life had become, the difficulty it began to inflict on me, and the sudden sense of emptiness I felt. Just when life was supposed to pay benefits to me, I was required to pay money, time, strength, and emotions for things I knew nothing about. What are these years exactly — the years I began to call "the tough years"? They comprise the season of life when the needs men have and the challenges they face in their families, their relationships, and their businesses are the greatest they have ever faced, while their capacity and resources to meet the needs and deal with these challenges dwindle.

The refinement of middle age can be brutal, not at all a simple polishing of the diamond, but more like a file or wire brush scraping rust off a weathered piece of steel. Men I knew weren't talking about their own journeys through this maze. Our kids were leaving home, disrupting our sense of family. Mirrors reflected wrinkles and stress lines. Work felt claustrophobic, the ironic sentence of self-inflicted choices made in the blissful ignorance of youth. Church became a boring and empty duty, as though some soul-devouring rodent were released to gnaw on my heart and my carefully constructed identity. I chafed against the chains that held me to my stump.

When men least expect it, at least for former optimists like me, times get tough. The years we think will be filled with peace and the satisfaction of our labors become the years of our greatest struggles and our deepest anxieties. Stubborn uncertainties swell to full-blown doubt. Children take paths leading them to pain and to life lessons they must learn. Our role is to watch and pray as sentries on the wall of the city and to be ready if the call for help comes.

No one told us of these years; no one prepared us. Not our fathers, not our friends, not our teachers, not our pastors, and certainly not the dream-making machinery, which convinced us while we were still small children that we could be anything we wanted to be. No one promised we would actually like whatever it was we would become if our dreams were to come true.

I left the farm in 1970 in search of my dreams with a noticeable chip on my shoulder, worked two years in construction, and quit before work one morning in September without notice. Something was wrong with the world, and I knew it. I have the greatest admiration for men who work on the assembly line, who devote thirty or forty years to our farms and factories, because their love and commitment to provide for their families are unflappable. Back then, I feared and despised such a life and knew I could never live that way. I was wired differently. I knew I was not destined to spend years or decades setting steel, pouring concrete, or working in what for me was a mindless routine day after day until my heart and the dreams within shriveled and died. But I shudder when an old school friend tells me about some of the things I said at the time. Arrogance, predictably, charges a great price for its indulgences.

A few months before my twenty-third birthday, I arrived in one of the great American dream worlds—Music City, USA. My plan was to be in Nashville for a year and then move on, establish some kind of business enterprise, become wealthy, have a family with approximately five kids, and live as every man deserves to live—admired and loved by everyone around me. Because of my success, I would be a respected man of the community, and my sons would sit with me among the elders at the city gate. As a man of strength, I would avoid the weaknesses common to other men. I would gain the esteem of others by wisely sidestepping mistakes that derail and destroy lesser men. My hand was strong on the rudder of my own destiny, so I waved my guardian angels good-bye.

One night I had a dream, the first of several vivid impressions with slivers of profound meaning even I was able to grasp. I was back on the farm, plowing in tall grass, driving the old John Deere. I stopped under a tree at the edge of the field to clear some branches, jumped off the tractor, took a few steps forward, and nearly stepped on a poisonous snake that was coiled and ready to strike. Just before it did, a branch fell from the tree and killed the snake. I called my mother to ask her what it meant. She said God was protecting me from danger, danger of which I was unaware and danger from which I was not capable of protecting myself. She said this was not a onetime experience but symbolic of how God would protect me as I learned to trust him with my life.

To say I lost my way as I pursued my own course is euphemistic at best. The truth is that I was a mess, absorbed in myself, bereft of the direction of older brothers except for one, proving that no man has what is required to live alone. The lonely days and nights cloaking my life like a shroud came with many voices, but not with many friends. One voice, which came from a man I mistook for a friend, convinced me to borrow some money and invest with him in a farm. In just a few years, he told me, we could sell the cattle and the land and have money to spare. I knew how to run a farm, he said, and we could hire someone to live there. What was there to lose? We would enjoy the delights of dreamers, the benefits without much work. It sounded like a way to outsmart the curse of Eden.

I was about to learn that life is like a stoked furnace. A praying mother and a God who loves you, combined with your own ignorance, will bring on the heat, possibly even a downturn in the real estate markets. There could not have been a more stupid time to invest in a dilapidated farm on a deserted Tennessee country road in the middle of nowhere. Or to expect Momma to like the girl I was dating. Or to think God did not care about the growing excesses of my life. Or to mistake camaraderie for friendship. The storm of destruction broke late one night when my friend and the girl informed me they were in love. He was filing for divorce from his family, and they were getting married. And by the way, she said, *they* would not be making even one more payment on the farm. It would be sold at auction in thirty days.

Betrayed by my friends, I spent the rest of that night in the barn, facedown, weeping until there were no more tears. Picture that: a prodigal son, a broken farm kid, facedown in barnyard residuals. The irony was not lost. God knows how to make the arrangements. In the long hours of the night, I came to realize God's will for me is *always* better than anything I ever choose for myself. God blessed me through those desperate circumstances. My weaknesses, I discovered, were not deal breakers with God; rather, they were the precise points where I experienced his greatest tenderness. In fact, honesty about my flaws would become a means of grace for others who needed to see whether Jesus is real, whether he has the power to authentically change a man or is nothing more than a dead Middle Eastern rabbi who serves the world as a compelling but ancient religious icon. When dawn broke after that long and weary night, I opened my eyes to the glory and beauty of the morning light, aware God was very near. He was at home in humble stables, and he had come to find his son.

God can use any circumstance, and he used treachery in others to create awareness and sorrow in me that led to valuable life changes. Nearly two years went by after the farm auction had left me deep in debt. Two years without a word of apology. Two years of leaning on what I learned in the barnyard dirt until I heard some "good news" that really ticked me off. These two scoundrels repented and gave their lives to the living Christ. Why would God be so nice to them, I complained? Why would he receive them? How dare he save *them*? If their faith was authentic, even slightly so, they would have apologized, come to me in humility and begged for forgiveness. So I reckoned they were fakes. But God was still dispensing my lesson.

Not long after, I discovered my "friends" were planning to attend a conference I was scheduled to attend in Indiana. I considered canceling but knew I could not because of various commitments, so I determined to avoid them no matter what. I arrived at the conference, drove my car to the lodge where I was to stay, and pulled my car into the one remaining parking spot—and *they* were sitting directly in front of me on a picnic table a few yards away. They spotted me before I could get the car in reverse and came running. I got out of the car. They threw their arms around me and begged me to forgive them. They told me they had come to faith and wanted to thank me, that I was the first person they ever met who they knew for sure was a Christ-follower. How could that be true, I asked, since these two knew *all* the sins of my prodigal years? They said they did not know how, only that they knew, and then I wept, disinvested of the lie that God expected me to hide my weaknesses from others. He could, in fact, use me more if I lived in truth than in half-truth or shadows. This was the third lesson of the first betrayal. If God would use a prodigal son like me for his purposes, life was going to be much more interesting than I imagined.

I tell this story from my youth because I assumed then that this one grand lesson taught me about as much as I needed to know. More than twenty years passed. God gave me a family, a wife well suited for tolerating my eccentricities, a practical thinker who loves people as much as I do and who actually knows how to balance a checkbook. The kids showed up and grew up, and the seeds of lifelong friendship were planted with three other couples whose lives became woven with ours through every kind of life experience you could name. Business grew and provided us the financial cover we needed, even in the midst of the ups and downs of entrepreneurial uncertainties. We experienced both the joys and sorrows of life. We learned more about our weaknesses and slowly learned to pray, "Your will be done," and "Do whatever you want to do in our lives to accomplish your purposes in us and through us." These are life-giving prayers spoken according to his will. He hears them, answers them, and by them creates otherwise impossible beauty. But they are also adventurous and disruptive, even dangerous if you think life on this broken planet is a mini version of the Promised Land and expect to paddle your canoe on a flat-water lake without wind or surprises, without the need for Jesus to come walking on your troubled waters to say, "Peace! Be still!" Our waters were still troubled.

The first betrayal was a furnace leading to repentance and, just as importantly, toward authenticity as a developing life pattern. The second betrayal was a consuming fire. The Scriptures say that God is "like a refiner's fire," that "he will purify the sons of Levi ... and they will bring offerings in righteousness to the LORD."[2] By the first betrayal and the one to follow, I discovered much about friendship — what it is and isn't, and what the Lord uses to refine my heart and the hearts of men. The first betrayal was difficult. God was present in each one, but the second and third were excruciating.

THE TOUGH YEARS

The tough years in a man's life show up like a bucket of snakes and weird crawling things. Whatever is in the bucket comes crawling out.

God prescribes fire for the gnarly critters that attach themselves to us. He knows just when to turn on the heat, just what spot to put us in so we cannot run from the purifying fire. We need our brothers more during the middle years than at any other season of our lives, because it is the time when men are most alone. These middle years are rough years when men have not yet learned to lean on each other in their shared weakness, when confident men begin to question themselves and everything

> **We need our brothers more during the middle years than at any other season of our lives, because it is the time when men are most alone.**

they believe. It is a time when men grow tired and restless and fearful or decide that because of their success they are invincible. It is a time when they face mystery and uncertainty unlike any other time during their lives. Although men seek to repurpose their lives during the middle years more than at any other time, it is also the season when men experience the greatest incident of betrayal. Perhaps it is because they have become weak and are easy prey, or have become targets because of their strength, or because God is using the mess of human relationships to accomplish something better than we could create for ourselves. Any way you look at it, betrayal by brothers feels like hell.

Several years after we moved into a new home, life was beautiful. The neighbors were all delightful and fun loving, and all the kids were above normal. Everything was as nice as a Garrison Keillor poem. We were creating a community, a safe and loving environment for our children, a place to nurture the dreams we created for those we loved—and we were proud of it. We were dedicated churchgoers celebrating our freedom from legalism and religion, but our hearts were not yet free. Perfection still had a grip on us.

Churches everywhere were promoting the idea of Promise Keepers, men's groups to change the world, and accountability groups promising to make everything about men better. Wives were happy "their men" were taking care of their stuff, and everyone knew what "their stuff" meant. It was a recipe for disaster, and the guys who met on our porch every Tuesday soon proved that the last great men's movement in America should have been named Promise Breakers. Sorry, Coach. We bring whatever we have to the game.

In a nutshell, one of the brothers with previous trouble keeping his pants zipped admitted to having a relationship with a younger woman. We implored him to give her up and to let us help him find a way back to healing with his wife and sons. We told him if he left the porch that sad morning, we would never see him again, not because we did not want to see him, but because his choices would lead him far away from us and from those who loved him. We told him the result of his choices would be that he would not feel welcome and loved around us, not because we would not welcome him or love him, but because that is the nature of bent and broken things. He said he was very sorry, but he got into his car and turned left toward the open highway, and we have rarely seen him since. The empty chair where our brother sat before he "fell off the porch" was full of sadness — but we did not go to find him, and we did not bring him home.

Conversations on Tuesday mornings continued to fill some gaps in our lives, but discernment was not our strength, and we did not know much about spiritual friendship. We were still lost in the paradigm of religious duties, systematic theology, and fixing what was broken instead of inviting Jesus to be present continually in the midst of our mess so we could be forgiven and healed rather than fixed. So when another friend on the porch told us of a dark inner fiend he could no longer control, we jumped into action and found a respected in-residence program in another state where, by God's mercy, he did receive healing and grace. His marriage was restored, his family was preserved, but a significant point about our life together was that he never did participate in the conversations on the porch when he returned home. It was a mystery then, but now I know why. It is because we did not live out of our weaknesses or understand authenticity. Perhaps we had none to offer, but the circumstances that followed seem now to have been designed to rid us of the shams and facades masquerading as modern spirituality. Ideas about church and Jesus flourished, but Jesus was not the center of our life together.

The porch group dwindled but was sputtering along until one day in June a few years later. Word came that one of our guys was arrested for various flagrancies while on vacation. He was in jail with threats on his life, and several friends were on their way to help him home. I was astounded and wrecked. Words could not describe what I felt. I never expected my brother to be perfect, but this was beyond my imagination. I thought I knew his struggles, but obviously I hadn't had a clue about the battle he fought and finally lost. The following Tuesday morning, I sat on my porch for a long time, groaning, alone as a man without friends is alone when there is no comfort.

Dark gravity won, and we fell off the porch one by one, broken by a magnitude reserved for those who try to make of this world a perfect home. Our experiment collapsed. The porch episodes were not personally directed from one brother toward the other, but even so, they left scars of the Judas kiss on family and friends. We betrayed our own ideal, unable to live up to it, and the collateral wreckage began. The worst sorrow of our lives together came a few years later as one friend denied his faith and tried to convince scores of people whom he had introduced to a relationship with Jesus Christ that everything, including God, was a farce. He is but one of the men who ravaged our city in those conflicted days, swapping one marred identity for another false self, exchanging the glory of God for the addictive pleasures of self-indulgence until he was captured by them. Some of us contributed to the devastation through our silence, while others resorted to renewed religious diligence. Young men were left flapping in the breeze, wondering what had happened to their fathers and spiritual leaders. "The tough years" arrived like a plague.

You could say ours were moral problems, and some of them were. Or that they were ethical affairs, and you would be right. Or twistings involving psychological and religious addiction disorders, and perhaps that is true. We had gotten to the place where systematic theology cannot help a man. Whatever hinge made the door swing, our porch group was a casualty, among other things, of faulty thinking and conversations that in hindsight seem mostly irrelevant. "Believe the best about others until given a reason not to" was as much a part of our philosophy of life as any biblical text. This cute little bit of social code, however, is the first step on the primrose path to spiritual blindness. What is true is always better. You can kiss friendship and porch groups good-bye if you live in a delusion that does not permit you to observe the truth about yourself and your peers. Leo Tolstoy, in his amazing novel *Resurrection*, says, "Men are like rivers: the water is the same in all."* Men share a common baseline, but I still did not know it. My journey in friendship had miles to go, but I was like a man walking in fog. I still spent time with men but enjoyed it less and less. Silence and sports chatter were the predominant forms of male communication all around me.

CRANKIN' UP THE HEAT

After we experience great sorrows and suffer the deafening noise of a complex world, God knows how to lead us to quiet streams, to give us rest before the next hard climb. For a year or so, things were quiet enough. The business grew, but I was empty and very tired of day-to-day pressures, so I delegated everything I could to a trusted staff at the office. On January 2 that year, I wrote three words: "alive and thirsty." One afternoon a few months later, I was walking through the meadow behind our home. Like lightning in my mind, the words Jesus spoke a few hours before Peter denied he even knew his best friend split the peaceful summer day. "Satan has asked to sift you as wheat. But I have prayed for you.... And when you have turned back, strengthen your brothers."[3] The interruption was real and personal. I stopped in my

---

* Leo Tolstoy, *Resurrection* (New York: Heritage, 1963), 174.

tracks and said, "No-ooooo! No-ooooo!" I contemplated Peter and the famous rooster, then added, "God, if this is really *you*, all I ask is the test not be so severe that I would deny you."

Whatever the refining fire accomplished, I was about to enter the forge, the place where life and death beat the hell out of you, the place God does not permit you to die, although you volunteer to do so. Nor does he leave your side, although you seldom feel his presence. Until now, I did not know how to forgive in the way Jesus means us to forgive each other. Could he really have meant we are to love malicious enemies, the ones who hurt us because they meant to do it, and to forgive brothers whose purpose is to destroy us? Dante, in his *Inferno*, reserves the lowest level of hell for betrayers of friends. Judas resides there, if that gives you a clue. That is precisely where I wanted to send those who would hurt me.

The third betrayal occurred in business with brothers I trusted with enough responsibility and authority to destroy what had taken nearly thirty years to build. Intrigue was their "new world order." Destructive debt-to-earnings ratios weakened the company and productivity languished while they created a shadow company to take over when mine failed. For more than a year, I dreaded going to the office to face exactly what, I did not know. A man sometimes knows something before he knows it, and I knew something was drastically wrong. The day after yet another tragic school shooting in which students died and families were swept into a category of grief they never bargained for, one of my associates walked into my office and said, "Another shooting. This will be good for business." I could not believe what I heard, and I knew business as usual had come to a screeching halt. I was leaving within hours to spend time with a dear friend who lost a daughter at Columbine, and the contrast between what I felt for him and his family compared to the devilish statement I just heard felt like the difference between heaven and hell. I was devastated.

A night or two after my return, three brothers, whose care I will never forget, showed up at my house and said, "We came tonight to talk about everything you have told us about your company. We sense things are worse than you think. We want you to tell us everything you know, everything you think is wrong, and we will help you translate what is really happening. We don't think you have much time to save your business." These brothers—my banker, my CPA, and a consultant—all knew our company well. I told them my suspicions, my fears, and the bits and pieces that pointed to disaster, including suspected banking irregularities, growing company debt, possible theft of proprietary intellectual property rights, and moral compromises. A few days later, the world I thought I had been living in fell apart. Recovered computer files confirmed for me a fact that became a lie: *men were not to be trusted.*

Dealing with the emotional turmoil was one thing and working through the near bankruptcy of my business was another, but forgiving guys who were my Christian brothers was the most difficult of all. Where I came from, men did not treat their enemies this way, and certainly not their brothers. More than two years passed as the pendulum of my soul swung from bitterness to forgiveness and right back again and again. I was trapped, and forgiving seventy times seven did not seem to help. How long would I be the pathetic creature spinning the wheel in the hamster cage of my mind? I never knew emptiness could be so empty. If I could not get off the wheel, I knew my soul would die.

Then at a men's retreat in New York, Jack Deere told the story of the man who was forgiven a huge mountain of debt he could not pay and was released from prison. Upon his release, he accosted a man who owed him a few hundred bucks and had him arrested. When the king who forgave him discovered his cruelty, he was thrown back into prison until he paid every cent of the debt. I had heard this story many times, but the next line, "So also my heavenly Father will do to every one of you, if you do not forgive your brother from your heart," was something I had never comprehended.[4] "What will your heavenly Father do to you?" Jack said. "You were forgiven and set free, but God will put you in a prison of your own making unless you forgive the brothers who have sinned against you." Completely forgiving the guys who hurt me was the last thing I wanted to do. In fact, I wasn't sure complete forgiveness was something I *could* do. But I was desperate, and facing a prison sentence from God for which I actually held the key for my own release was the perfect ambush. Talk about sneaky Jesus! Only God can simultaneously make a man both a prisoner and his own jailor inside a prison of his own making. I made my choice. With God's help, I would forgive from my heart all offenses, then and in the future. That cold winter evening, I knelt down in front of God and three hundred men, confessed my bitterness and inability to forgive, and asked an old man to pray for me. He laid his weathered hands on my head and prayed. I wept, gave up my pride, forgave, and received pardon. From that night on, I was a free man. I am only sorry it took me so long.

So here's the deal. If a man can be self-condemned, he can certainly be self-imprisoned. If it is possible to be self-incarcerated, it is also possible, with an ambush by God and a little help from your friends, to be set free. When we are hurt, the bait to return to prison looks and smells like justice, although it is merely our desire for revenge. Holding on to our hurts ensures the wounds we have endured will not heal. Rick Wienecke, the noted Israeli sculptor, has said, "We need someone to disturb the relationship [between us and our wounds] to bring healing." That person could be your wife or a wise parent, your only friend, a complete stranger, Jack Deere, or an old man who confers blessings on the heads of the sorrowful with worn-out hands, or anyone who knows how to stand in for Jesus at the point of your need. God is very good at setting captives free, so beware of him if you prefer revenge and living inside the security of your own prison. Out here, there is a God on the loose, and he is good.

My personal failures toward my brothers, looking back, were greater than I realized at the time. I tried to delegate my calling from God to them because I was tired, placing a burden on them that was not theirs to carry instead of working to help them discover their own passions. I expected them to participate in my dreams and my success but was slow to consider their dreams. That they became bitter toward me is sad, but not a surprise; in fact, it is not something I hold against them. We were all learning—the hard way.

"The tough years" deliver enormous challenges, including changes in family structures as children leave home, as death and divorce take their tolls, as job security fades, as once minor weaknesses compound to deliver disproportional consequences, as disappointments and expectations about life collide and create nuclear reactions, and as physical realities and health issues challenge the authenticity of spiritual life. In the face of such uncertainty, more than a few men I know have resorted to desperate measures. Rather than accepting the journey of this life for what it is, in which God promises to be always present with his people, they still look for a Promised Land on earth—but they will not find it. There is a popular idea that says men need to move from success to significance, but I believe every little bit of life is significant. Nothing is wasted—not the mundane or the great social and spiritual enterprises, not even the years spent chasing your own tail—if you will stop long enough to receive wisdom and grace reserved in your name by your Life Designer.

Until a man forgives the offenses against him, he does not and truly cannot understand himself or other men.

Forgiveness generates an essential framework of understanding about the nature of men. Until a man forgives the offenses against him, he does not and truly cannot understand himself or other men. Man is by nature a life giver, and refusing to forgive is a self-fulfilling death wish, the ultimate suffocation of the emotional and spiritual wellspring of our own identity. Forgiveness is a deep cool stream in which the water is cool enough to soothe the heat of anger among brothers and quench the fires of hell among archenemies.

Jesus was the first and only God to die on a cross, chiefly so enemies could become friends. No other figure has or ever will make a more declarative statement while suffering. "Father, forgive them" split human history forever into two groups, two kinds of people: those who forgive and are forgiven and those who will not forgive and are not forgiven.[5] The greatest moral choice a man will make arrives on the point of his enemy's sword.

The exquisite truth, a recurring narrative I once despised but now love with all my heart, is that God loves betrayers and the betrayed equally. God does not measure our sins or weigh them as a mathematical equation. God loves me as much as those I have harmed, and he loves those who have wounded me just as much while they were hurting me as he did while I was being hurt. Only when we know this can we stop ruining each other. Only when we receive such amazing love from our Father do we even want to. Whatever your circumstances, lean into his arms. He will help you through the tough years, and in the end, he will take you safely home.

But this story is not yet complete—not quite. Nearly a decade later, one of my former associates, in his own swamp of circumstances that are remarkably similar to those I faced earlier, came to ask me, a few months ago, how long it had taken me to get over my anger. He wondered if I had been able to forgive them—before or after I had gotten out of debt. In our own *Les Misérables* way, we are on a path to restore our relationship as brothers, and I suspect we will spend the rest of our years reversing the effects of our previous irritations and discontent, as if by design.

TEN

SADNESS IN THE CHURCH

"WHAT'S YOUR AGE IN CHURCH YEARS?" my friend Jimmy asked me recently.

"What do you mean?" I replied, thinking he was talking about life in cat or dog years or the biblical phrase that to God a thousand years "are but as yesterday."[1] I've been in church all my life, so I was thinking I must be in the millions.

"If you live in legalism and tradition," he said, "you live in an accelerated aging process. If you live in spirit and in truth, you are forever young."

By 1973, the traditional American church, like a tired old boxer, was on the ropes. We did not know it at the time, but we were. Two world wars, the Korean War, and the insanity of Vietnam called to question every assumption about tradition and our way of life as Americans. So did Elvis, the Beatles, the beatniks, Haight-Ashbury, Dr. Martin Luther King Jr., abortion rights, the Cold War, the folk prophets, Watergate, and free sex. The rumblings of a society reordering itself pierced the night.

Outside the church, naïveté took a knockout punch. Many traditional churches chugged blissfully along but had lost much of their cultural and human relevance. The lights were down and nearly out, and Elvis had left the building. The Jesus Movement, rejected by the establishment religion, seemed for many the only part of the peaceable kingdom visible to us, or the only thing that made any intellectual or practical theological sense. It was also about the only voice outside the church saying, "Jesus loves you no matter who you are, no matter what you have done." Otherwise night had come, and the cute little church was fast asleep. Saying "Jesus loves you" outside the building, believe it or not, sounded revolutionary—and it was. It still is.

In search of God during the Watergate era when she was seventeen, my wife, Linda, went with a friend to a Sunday service somewhere in Orange County, California, hoping "to find God and figure out why he was bugging me and keeping me awake at night." The preacher went into a political rant about Nixon and corruption in Washington. But somehow he forgot to talk about God. Not one to bless a fool with her presence, Linda whispered to her friend that she wanted to leave and stood up, hoping to slip quietly down the aisle and outside. The minister, his sermon interrupted, demanded to know where they were going. Linda stopped, turned around to face the congregation, and said to him, "Well, I came to find God, but he is not here." Little old ladies fanned themselves to keep from fainting, while his rant, this one against her, rose a good octave or two. She did what all smart children do in the face of a bully—she ran. That her search for God continued may be something of a miracle.

Liberal churches preached about social justice and civil rights, against Nixon, and used God to prove that it was OK to kill babies and that it was their obligation to stop nukes. While "the liberals" were energizing the fans of little old ladies and doing some honest work in social justice, conservative churches preached against abortion, rock music, and every other sin they knew, real and imagined. It was wrong to kill babies but all right to use nukes to defend our freedom. Jesus was their backup man, the copilot for emergencies they could not handle themselves. These were the days when the church was confused, each sect having a miniature of the truth, a little automatic Jesus waiting in the prayer closet at our beck and call. One side of the aisle worshiped freedom, while the other worshiped freedom of choice. Church attendance declined.

The language of entitlement entered the church, the invention of words and phrases such as *protest, moral majority, political power, a seat at the table, invitation to the White House, my meeting with the president, boycott, culture war, choice, liberal media, gender conflict, activist, Christian right, Christian left,* and a host of other words and ideas not found a single time in the sacred Scriptures of the Christian faith. On our way back to Egypt, we constructed another tower in the plain of Shinar and did not know what language we were speaking. The interpreters in the bully pulpits behind these movements began telling us what to think and how and when to think it, so we did. We did not perceive what it would do to us and to our children, or what it would do to the light that shines in the darkness. Before it was over, we lost our minds, our hearts, and our souls to the cares of this world, and some of us did not know Teletubbies could not be gay because they are only dolls. (An entire news cycle reported on this awkward headline from the "kingdom of God.") We were like the virgins whose lamps had burned out in the dark of night for lack of oil. This was the beginning of the self-absorbed Christian industrial complex. We, not our children, were the original Entitlement Generation.

MAKING THE CHURCH IRRELEVANT

With straight faces, our leaders called men and women to dedicate their lives to this insanity, and the church became cultlike, asking its members to give everything to the cause, like a failed Sun Myung Moon, instead of giving to the flock as the good shepherd did when he gave his life for the sheep. The sorrow of the late-twentieth-century church in America is that we listened to these men and their little ideas, men who discovered the way to raise money was to stir up hatred and controversy through the stream of bad news reported in their newsletters, on their TV programs, and from their pulpits. Good news isn't good for fund-raising, and we were separated from everyone with whom we could not agree. The Godhead, we were told, was well pleased with us, but I do not remember any doves descending, and I cannot say there was a voice from heaven.

Adding to our conflicted sense of well-being was the thought that evil would soon be crushed by our efforts, and with God as our helper we would usher in the return of the Messiah and the coming millennium of peace. If the suffering church has the distinction of doing this, that's one thing, but the plump American church? More than one bestselling author predicted the Messiah would return by 1997, lending fuel to the religious train heading away from meaningful involvement in the arts and culture, the gifts God gives to make joyful the hearts of men. Leave it to the American church of the last century to devise the idea of a "suffering-free" escape for all true believers. The hungry and suffering church in Africa and around the world, to this day, has no such illusion.

With this renewal of separatism came a near-rabid preoccupation with cultural disengagement. We would discover, but not quickly enough, that the eschatology of our imagination is not the eschatology of the Bible. "Left behind" is a remarkable description of the great loss and effect of this disconnection between the church and general society. The harm done to both is still not fully understood by either. What a man believes can be observed in what he does. One who does not receive the whole counsel of God does not live in the real world, whether he is a churchman or not. In King James terms, the order of Jesus to his followers was to "occupy" until his return, and he was not speaking of a military occupation or a culture war.[2] Living the mundane routines with courage, creating from the *imago Dei* within, loving our neighbors as we love ourselves, following Jesus Christ instead of arrogant religious leaders, and making do with truth and light could have improved our schools and neighborhoods far more than our strategies to "take cities for Christ."

We were little, but then we became big and outgrew our britches. The observing world beheld our nakedness, which we denied—we said all they were seeing was a new kind of cloth we had made ourselves. We believed if we could prove the truth, the whole world would run to it and be saved. Some hoped a biblical worldview, or the kindly ghettos we created, would save our prodigal children—but only Jesus cares enough about them to do that. While we were doing all these things, we developed the ability to transform the most life-changing message in the universe to a sleep-inducing soliloquy on the evils of the material world and the ever more distant glories of heaven. In doing so, we were barely Christian at all. Our strategies and delusions led to a massacre, the death of joy.

Our causes remained well funded. Our missions and some of our government offices were staffed with believers, and truth hung like trophies on our structured systems of theology until they collapsed under the weight of our pride. But we did not know we were proud, only that it was our turn to walk in the halls of power. Into this chaos comes Jesus riding on a donkey, suffering once again the humiliation of his wayward children, offering to become one of the least of these while they cheer him and yet refuse to follow him in suffering, death, and resurrection. Very few want to be least in the kingdom.

G. K. Chesterton observed that Christianity has died many times only to be resurrected again, for it had a God who knew the way out of the grave, which should give us something to celebrate.[*] What does the church in the world look like? What is the kingdom of heaven on earth? Why do we care more about politics in Washington than we do about Jesus, more about our agenda than kindness to our neighbors? Why are we more angry at our ideological opponents than we are at our own apathy, and why do we neglect to bring others the gifts of the presence of Christ, gifts that are at once spiritual and material and actually do have the power to change the world?

RESURRECTING HOPE AND COMMON SENSE

Pull back for a while from all of this and take another look at the followers of Jesus. Get your eyes off religious politics, off yourself, off the current excesses and omissions of the church in America, and look at

---

[*] G. K. Chesterton, *The Everlasting Man* (London.: Hodder & Stoughton, 1947), 290.

the global church. There are brothers and sisters in every part of the world, among all peoples and tribes, every language group, every size and shape, every color and smell, educated and not, under the bridges and in the high towers of civilized society, in prisons and hospitals, on deathbeds or hungry, sleeping on thin mats in huts and under the open skies—everywhere in the uttermost parts of the world. There are 2.3 billion of us who call ourselves followers of Jesus. Our individual and collective prayers ascend day and night to the one who hears and knows what to do with our cares and with us. As out of control as the world is on any given day, as disconnected as his children are from him on some days, I've never seen God worried, anxious, or afraid. He could, however, be a bit ticked at our failure to love and care for others—and you might want to think about that.

Did you ever wonder why God's strategy to save the world, when you think about it, seems almost stupid? Take you, for example, or any of us. Everyone who has lived before us is dead. We're all he has, and for some delightful reason he loves us and wants us and thinks we are his children. As someone said, he has given us a few errands to do while we are here. What seems really crazy to me is that he has placed his strategy for saving the world into our care for our few remaining years on earth, and then he is going to hand it to a whole new batch of kids, who are just as messed up as we are. I'm just sorry my generation wasted so much time in religious movements, pretending it wasn't messed up as it jockeyed for political influence, as though that has ever made much of anything measurably better for the long term.

I'm also sorry we are such a joyless bunch, barely convinced we are loved. This is our greatest weakness, our deepest sadness—so deep and sad we can barely say it aloud. I've been asking church people for a long time if they know many Christians who are filled with joy. Nearly everyone shakes his head and gets a sad look deep in his eyes. It seems to me that a man who knows he is loved is joyful. He will do just about anything for his lover, full of gratitude for the opportunity. A man who is unsure of love acts in anger and must lose himself in a cause or a set of rules to find a sense of identity. I believe our modern political-religious movements will die with their leaders, and I do not believe the recent batch deeply believed they were loved by God. Their actions so often betrayed them. Their words were angry and distorted, and what they hoped to accomplish through a movement could have been done in half the time with a tenth of the funding if this great love of Jesus had been more visible in every part of their lives. If Christ is in us, then I am afraid we have done an amazing job of blurring his love, joy, peace, patience, kindness, and the other evidences of his presence others should easily see.

> **A man who knows he is loved is joyful. He will do just about anything for his lover, full of gratitude for the opportunity.**

The kingdom of God must become the first priority very soon or the church of the twenty-first century in the West will fail to rise above the mediocrity and oblivion of the politically charged late-twentieth-century church. Any congregation that fails to make the kingdom its clear priority is irrelevant. The church in America is showing some signs of life, and it would be naive to write it off, but the next movement in and through the church will not be political, nor will it be another "be good enough for God to love you" society. Whatever shape or form the church takes, it will be a church filled with God's presence. The real Jesus will be welcomed and will be the center, while our dumbed-down versions of the great I AM disappear like froth on an after-church latte. With Christ as the center, may the male domination and the feminization of the church both be damned.

FINDING HEALING AFTER RELIGIOUS RATIONALISM

I don't know if we can do it. Can liberal Christians never say that war *and* abortion are wrong? Can conservative believers confess that nationalism gets in the way of the kingdom of God? Can we not agree to unite our hearts to fear his name by serving the needs of the poor, visiting those in prisons, caring for the homeless, inviting broken families to our dinner tables to receive healing, infusing ourselves as salt and light into every sector and corner of society, involving ourselves in our local schools so children may have a better education than government programs alone could ever provide? Can we make sure every business deal we control is fair, and then worship together around the common table, where we all admit we are sinners as we share sacred bread and holy wine in the presence of Jesus? What is the business of the kingdom except caring for people, bringing them good news, and becoming for them and for ourselves brothers who were once lost but are now found?

I'm not against the church in any way. I'm for it, I'm part of it, and I love it. I mean, I love the people, but like you, I am *not* for a church making up its own game, content to sit and stare at performers or to listen to hash from www.sermons.com that anyone can buy with a credit card, with or without Internet ordination papers. Good enough, perhaps, for the "Dress Up for God Club," but I'd like something a little less contrived.

The great sadness is seeing how many men find church to be boring and how disconnected they are from other brothers, as well as the fact that we who are the church have not been with them or for them during their greatest struggles. It seems, in fact, that we do not know how, or do not care enough, to be there for each other in this entity we call "the body of Christ." We have pastors who have never worked outside vocational ministry trying to connect with our day-to-day struggles and church leaders who don't have close friends and wouldn't know what to do with a friend if they had one. Even today, many churches teach that our daily work isn't as important as "the work of the ministry," while applause rises for those who "surrender to full-time Christian service." If there is a crock of heresy being dumped on men, try that. The message is that friendship isn't really that important, and anything less than being a missionary or senior pastor just doesn't measure up. Too bad. Plumbers and lawyers, farmers and schoolteachers, assembly line workers and nurses, tech guys and trash men—they just don't measure up in God's hierarchy. I'm still for tarring and feathering any preacher who so much as infers that God is more pleased with "professional Christians" than the rest of us. The men I know are looking for brothers and fathers. They don't need or want another cause handed to them, another national campaign, another plan to fix men, another promise to keep, another big religion deal, or spiritual propaganda of any kind. They don't need more shame- and guilt-based methods. The mission of the kingdom, articulated by Jesus, is enough for a man, his friends, his neighbors, and his family to last a lifetime. The Italians have a word for *enough* that sounds quite amazing when you say it with emotion: *basta!* Meanwhile we're a little like Noah's ark after forty days of rain, locked up with all of creation's animals and no place to go. We're more than a little stinky but still rocking on through the storm, safe but a little stupid from all the fumes.

We have misconstrued Jesus' telling us we must "be perfect, as your heavenly Father is perfect" as an agenda we can accomplish here on earth.[3] I hear it almost every week from some corner of the Christian ghetto. Only arrogant people believe they no longer sin, and the Most Humble One who said these words surely did not give us a blessing or instruction that would lead to arrogance. What did he mean, then, to "be perfect" like our Father? If this refers to our performance, *we all fail*, and the words of Jesus may just as well have been left unsaid. But if he meant we should develop a heart like the Father's heart, that we should accept the work of Jesus to make us complete so we can relax and live out of the life we find in the Father's heart, then we have a fighting chance that it is possible to be perfect in that way— continually becoming perfect in love, one step at a time, because *he* is our source and not ourselves. The perfection of our Father to which Jesus calls us is *his perfect love*, not the idea that we are expected to, or even could do, everything right. I can barely get anything exactly right, and what a joy it is not to worry about it.

Living in the presence of Christ means at least one more thing—and living as kingdom people depends on it. One of the most counterintuitive statements our Lord ever made does not describe very well the day-to-day perspective of almost anyone I know: "My grace is sufficient for you, for my power is made perfect in weakness."[4] Now how about that? We spend our lives telling each other to focus on our strengths, to work in our core skill sets, to dance with the thing that brought us to the party, to perfect our brand, and to protect our image. This is not the beginning of an argument to tell you not to use your strengths, but it is to say that if you want to see the power of God at work in your life, you'll have to quit hiding your weaknesses from people and from him—as though you can hide anything long enough to actually get it past God or even the people who know you. It really just means you have to be honest, to deal in truth rather than fiction. This is the requirement of Jesus that scares the hell out of most Christians.

THE NEW STRATEGY TO CHANGE THE WORLD: BECOME A FRIEND OF JESUS

Can you imagine a church not obsessed with shame-based confession but filled with friends of Jesus who are completely unashamed to tell the truth about themselves? I know a few people like that, and they are refreshing to be with, unguarded enough to be present, wise enough to know when to speak and when to be silent, and truly at peace, whatever the mess in them and around them may be. Self-delusion is one of the more insidious propensities of our humanity, and being free of it is surely worth the price you pay for the cure.

Not only is God smart; he is clever enough to actually pull off this "body of Christ" thing. He built failure into the system by placing me and you next to each other, along with all the other imperfect friars in the class. He gives us an incredible gift called eternal life, and then with a smile on his face, he plops us next to each other and tells us to work it out, get along, get over ourselves, act like a family until you become one, invite other messed-up brothers to join in, and keep him at the center of our lives. If you want freedom, just accept this as the new normal. For the better part of two thousand years, it has actually worked—and it still does work, despite church wars and culture wars and other devilish battles we and our forebears created and fought because we forgot a thing or two Jesus told us.

Jesus is a wine maker, and making his wine is one of the kindest things he ever does. He created for his purpose grapes and people who like the juice, and the wine he created in Cana was just the beginning. People who attended that wedding said that this man, unlike other hosts, served his best wine last. The sheer volume of wine created that day was amazing, but so is the lesson to quit worrying about impressing others, to refrain from presenting the best things about yourself first—a nice idea the church should consider. Wine is for the celebration of life, used at the Last Supper and in the church through the holy sacrament for two millennia to bind his followers to himself in celebration of his presence among us. That he, the Wine Maker, said he would "not drink again of this fruit of the vine until that day when I drink it new with you in my Father's kingdom" is a pure delight.[5] The party will not begin without us. That many in the evangelical church have reduced Holy Communion to quick gulps of juice and bits of cracker borders on insane. Holy Eucharist should instead be at once both a somber repentance and a wild and joyful celebration of life. It is meant to be a means of grace by which we enter into his joy. Instead, for many, it is just another dull religious routine. "Move it along so we can get on with the rest of the service." May God save us from destruction!

I suppose the time is coming when most of the megachurches will have morphed into something more human friendly, when Oklahoma's disproportionate share of bad church architecture will have returned to the dust, when seminaries will quit destroying the only basis of their authority, and when pastors who have no friends begin to trust their brothers once again. I reckon this will not be tomorrow or the next day. We did not suddenly arrive in this condition, and it will take a magnificent work on the part of Jesus and his friends to turn the church back to what it was and should be—men and women without guile, sharing what they have like little children content to sit with Jesus and to let him do his work in and through us, loving the world to himself. This will happen as brothers whose hearts are made alive reserve to themselves the privilege of infecting others with love, joy, peace, patience, kindness, goodness, faithfulness, gentleness, and self-control, the true evidence of the presence of the Holy Spirit in their lives.[6] Remember, God is attracted to children and to adults who become like children.

May these qualities of the spirit of Christ shine through you, dear brothers, as good as fruit ripening on a tree, made possible by the kindness of the one who loves you so much.

That he trusts you with his gifts and with the least of these speaks well of you.

ELEVEN

BUILD YOUR OWN COFFIN

IMMIGRANTS FROM EUROPE IN THE MID-1700S must have been profoundly courageous. Without Skype, instant global messaging, email, jet planes, or the means to return to their homes, they left friends and family in the villages and farmlands of their birth and sailed west in little ships on the high seas toward an elusive dream. Many of them also left persecution and poverty for the promise of religious freedom and free land from William Penn. Our Swiss and German fathers found their new home in Big Valley, where Dad spent the first twenty-one years of his life during the Roaring Twenties and the Great Depression. Big Valley wasn't roaring then or now, and it still looks like a quiet little slice of Switzerland.

Imagining Dad as an Amish boy when he was our age, my brothers and I loved to explore the barns and buildings around the old homestead — a summer kitchen built with fieldstone and rock from the mountain quarry, a whitewashed 1800s-era stable in constant use, and a rickety but functional outhouse right there in the backyard, with a stack of pages from an old Sears catalog. We marveled at the odd convenience. One afternoon on a hike with Dad to the top of Jacks Mountain, my brothers discovered a remarkable fossil of a snake resting there on that old mountaintop waiting for us to discover it ever since the Great Flood. I had never heard of such a thing, a snake trapped inside a rock, and while the ark was nowhere in sight, Noah seemed very close. I suddenly felt like Peter and John on the Mount of Transfiguration and wished we could build a little hut and stay right there forever. Such is the desire of sons to be with their fathers. It is one of my first memories of longing.

Growing up in the dirt of agrarian America at the beginning of the twentieth century was not unusual, but being Amish has always been out of step with the rhythm and currents of the general population. If you had known my grandfather, you might have thought his contrarian streak was intentional, and it probably was. To us, his DNA was a complexity we understood. Members of groups who intentionally set themselves apart from a larger society can be both highly individualistic and yet participants in a social enterprise in which healthy community produces an unusual refinement of the whole. This tension creates, at one and the same time, a charming sense of humor and an almost serene grumpiness. In these communities, individual distinction has limitations. Not included in the list of Amish limitations are skilled craftsmanship, storytelling, intelligent farming, animal husbandry, mechanical inventions, culinary skills, high-quality homemade everything, and a variety of antics whose only purpose is to put a smile on the faces of neighbors and friends. My grandfather, having finished a new chimney on his two-story farmhouse, for example, proceeded to stand on his head on top of the chimney. Great uncles in my mother's family hid the buggy of their sister's boyfriend on the barn roof one evening when he came to visit. This is the beautiful lunacy of which legacies are made.

Nighttime at Grandpa's house was magical and mysterious. The night sounds of the farm, the gentle mooing of the calves, the cooing of pigeons in the barn, and the mournful whip-poor-wills called to us and to each other as we drifted off to sleep. With its oddity of old-fashioned chamber pots in every bedroom, soft wooden floors with two hundred years of creaks and memory, and smells of quilts, Grandpa's house made everything feel safe. Roosters, rude and ignorant as alarm clocks, woke everyone before the sun came up—before even God was awake—but the smell of Grandma's old-fashioned farmer breakfast was already in the air. Grandma's ancient wood-burning oven was a steady source of sweetness, and an old tin cup swung off a faucet that delivered cold mountain springwater right into her kitchen. In Big Valley, memories flood over me like the scent of lilac in spring. In the corner behind the bedroom door, Grandpa's homemade plywood coffin stood like a silent soldier of death. I'd forget it was there until the next visit, but it was always a frightful sight, flickering there in the corner by the light of a kerosene lantern when we closed the bedroom door at night. It was an eerie reminder that Grandpa knew he was going to die. He did not know when, and he wasn't sick until much later, but he knew death would come and did not seem to mind or to fear it. He was an original old-timer, unconcerned by social norms or his own eccentricities. Over the complaints of the undertaker, he insisted his body be hauled in the back of a pickup truck to the church and to his grave. He wasn't much for riding in black limousines or putting beautiful wood boxes into holes in cemeteries. Asked why there were not two coffins upstairs, whether he didn't think Grandma would need one, he smiled for a split second and said he could always build another if she needed it first. But she did not.

The day we buried Grandpa was cold and crisp. An ice storm swept the valley while we slept, and whether there was ever a prettier scene in Narnia, no one could say. Every twig and branch along both mountain ridges shone like the purity of heaven. Blazing bright against the blue, blue sky these ridges were a fare-thee-well and a welcome home as we pondered destiny, and hope, and God. We, farmers, people of the dirt, sang a hymn and with tender strength closed his grave, as has always been the custom in our family. For us, it is the last loving thing on earth a working man can do for his father or friend. We do not permit uncircumcised philistines to close the graves of those we love. We do not believe in earthmovers or callous gravediggers or mechanical Crank-a-tons used for the instant burial of the dead. When we laid Abraham Yoder's body in the grave, it was a gentle, careful, and loving good-bye, one shovelful at a time for an old Amish patriarch who had fought the good fight and finished his race. His spirit had already flown to Jesus past the bluebird sky, and he was a free man.

DIE SO YOU CAN LIVE

Everyone who has ever lived is dead, with the possible exception of those who are still alive. Otherwise, it's 100 percent. For this reason, and because we dread the unknown, death holds the power of great fear over us, so it is paradoxical that Jesus used his own death to set men free from the one who had the power of death. Having given his own life for our freedom, he issues us a sacred invitation to die to all iniquity so we can enjoy the gifts of life he has reserved for us in his name. Men want to know the agenda for everything we are asked to do before we agree to do it — so much so that when Jesus says a man must lose his life to find it and carry his own cross around as a reminder to die so he can live — without giving us all the details — there are not many takers. Doing what Jesus did sounds like a bad proposition, but seldom does the host spell out for his invited guests all the pleasures he has planned for a wonderful evening among friends. The problem for most men is that, until we really screw things up, we like ourselves pretty much the way we have made ourselves to be, and we are not deeply interested in the invitation of Jesus — a little detail not lost on the rest of the population. The risk of losing who we are or everything we have worked for all our lives is not the game we want to play. Giving it all up intentionally seems worse, a transaction we can do without.

Even so, men want to live — really live — and the world of men turns on this little grain of truth. The internal axis for everything a man does is powered by his desire for life, to not miss what he desires and deserves but make it his own before it passes him by. Not so long ago, *carpe diem* sounded so strong. It was just right for a twentieth-century fad, and it tickled our ears whenever we said it, sort of like

Roman soldiers ordering everyday citizens to carry their bags a mile down the road. But who knew what it meant? Like a perfect dream sequence that rolls over the senses like honey but smells and feels like dust left in my hand when I compel life to serve me, so *carpe diem* was just another stab at fulfilling our own longings. Living to take from life anything and everything you can destroys the very thing designed to give you pleasure, forcing what might be freely given if only there was love.

Before I wash the crud of my own selfishness away, I am sure I hate Solomon and his book of Ecclesiastes for being so right. How could everything I want be vanity? Seize the coffin, seize the cross, but do not ask me to take from life what is not mine when I am finally clean. Loving life and seizing life are two very different operations. When Jesus asks a man to receive life God's way—that is, to embrace the death of his own crud and to bear his own cross in order to live—he is asking him to make a choice to live in relationship with God while giving up and giving back what he has seized for himself. This is the choice that marks the fork in the road for all men, a choice that leads a man into meaningful relationships with others or reinforces a forlorn determination to go it alone. And the go-it-alone road has been overcrowded for a very long time.

JESUS LOVES THE DEAD AND DYING

A superior premise for life begins with this: Jesus was not crazy, and he has some extraordinary news for men. The good news is he cares supremely about relationships, including those with scoundrels, prostitutes, addicts, hypocrites, commoners, keepers of dark and hidden secrets, and cheats and losers of every stripe—even traitors who betray him with a kiss of friendship. There is plenty of evidence for this. What is extraordinary is that the death Jesus invites us to embrace somehow makes it possible to receive, quite literally, everything we need to actually *be* alive. Jesus guarantees he will make our hearts live. In fact, King David's prophetic description of the suffering liberator transitions from the mockery of onlookers, the dividing of his garments, and the piercing of his hands and feet to a victorious canticle of praise that contains one of the greatest celebratory blessings ever written. That blessing, "May your hearts live forever!" has become the frequent and favorite toast around our dinner table, and it is fitting around the table of the bread and the wine, as we remember Jesus and speak his name to our brothers.[1]

Jesus is like the farmer who knows that the seed he plants in the ground will die but that what follows will become valuable. Even one grain of truth can produce the prosperity of abundant freedom. Building your own coffin, then, is a metaphor to describe the spiritual attitude it takes to allow yourself to be buried by the Gardener of Eden so you can be resurrected and enter the community of life. It illustrates how you play your part as one of those refined and individual men who have laid down the heavy burden in exchange for one that is easy and light. The way of voluntary death leads to a restored community in which we receive joy and rest for our souls. Rest from the weary pursuit of self-gratification. Rest from the malignant emptiness and sorrows of our ill-tended manhood. Rest from performance and the bargains we have struck with false ideas and ideals that led us to our grief. Some say the way of Jesus is violent because he requires this kind of death and does not spare us from physical death, but the dying, if Grandpa was right, is almost as nonchalant as the planting of a new crop. The difficulty depends entirely on how much we resist the inevitable, or comprehend it as a new way to live.

If the way of Jesus is not violent, it is at least invasive. There is no getting away from it once you belong to him. When I awake each morning, I am greeted with two thoughts: *Oh, no, not again!*, which has much to do with how men approach the toil and doubts of our existence and the dread of a continuous struggle; the other is, *Oh, you're still here?*, as though God would skip out on me while I slept, like a lover paid to seize the night. Religion, which encourages the idea that we must earn our way to God, is exactly like that—mitigating the purity of God's sacred kindness to make him the ultimate quid pro quo. If you think or live as though God will desert you for a more capable, less flawed guy who can pay him more than you can pay, produce more good than you can produce, and earn more favor than you can earn, you are still imprisoned in a "God is my prostitute" state of mind. This deadly idea about God must die, and the quicker, the better. If you are still trapped inside the awful paradigm of religious performance, I'm advising you to get on with building your coffin right now. You've got a truckload or two of stuff that needs to be hauled to the cemetery, and soon. Perhaps some of our spiritual leaders in need of personal reformation could lead the caravan.

Religious perfection is not the only thing in men that needs to die and be buried forever. We need a good old Irish wake for all the stuff in our lives that keeps us a fraction of the men God made us to be. Our wake should celebrate the death of self-sufficiency and self-dependence, insecurity and rejection, all the bondage that comes from lies and half-truths, addictions to which we have submitted ourselves, threats, intimidation, power trips, abuse, greed, arrogance, lying, and pride. While you're at it, place all your fears in that old wooden box too. Go ahead. Get all the garbage out of your heart. A heart that is only half alive is little better than a dead heart. We are all going to die before long, no matter what we do to prevent it, and the moment we die, we will have lost it all—the good, the bad, and the ugly. Why not exchange the garbage you've been holding on to that has created the death and dying in your heart and voluntarily join the community of life instead of waiting to lay it down until your last breath is squeezed from you. Those of us who walk with Jesus know some things die easily while others take a lifetime. But having buried even the fear of death, with its lifelong bondage, we come to know that the gentle graces of Christ are sufficient for us in this new way of life, one day at a time. We do not need to seize anything. Instead, we joyfully receive with open hands the daily gifts offered to us.

THE ELEGANT DANCE OF LIFE

Before we can receive the benefits of those who live as sons of the Father, we must understand that one major element is missing in our lives together. We are gradually losing—and in many places have completely lost—the saving grace and kindness of a living and vibrant community of faith. While the societal pendulum has swung from rugged individualism to group twitters and tweets and other pop-tech nonsense, the unique individual characteristics of manhood and distinctive community alike have diminished. Because of this we are impoverished and barely know it, much less know what to do about it. And what good is it if this generation and each one to follow becomes more passive in everything except in the pursuit of our own satisfaction and entertainment and forgets what our Master said—that only those who do the will of our Father are his brothers and may enter the kingdom of heaven.

Community as I know it and saw it lived in the simplicity of the Amish and Mennonites is best described as a *common unity*, a communing unity held together as one by a shared desire for life to be complete, to be filled with love, heritage, faith, and gentle goodness. We knew what many church groups and social clubs never discover, namely, that families are more valuable than success, children are more important than sports, Grandma and Grandpa in their frailty could not be sent away to die unless medical conditions required it, working together for the good of another does more to build a community than another round of golf, hardship creates a better life than a regular schedule of parties, and God enjoys and blesses our celebration of his goodness. We were gentle with each other, and we sought the good of our brothers above our own benefit. We held others in higher esteem than we did ourselves. We practiced the saying "Let another praise you" and considered how not to think of ourselves more highly than we ought to think.[2] We forswore all lawsuits and practiced forgiveness of all men and every offense, asking and giving mercy freely, and when we received the Lord's Supper, we knelt in humility before each other to wash our brothers' feet. We would keep our promises, even if it hurt us to do so. I do not think Mennonites or Amish are more perfect than any other group of people on earth, but one thing they know better than most is how to create a community of faith that cares for the least member as though he or she were the greatest. In this celebration of the weak, they are examples of Jesus Christ our Savior.

Community, for me, is a powerful word that describes the celebration of the dead who have experienced the power of the resurrection, who because of mercy have given up all thought of being good enough for God and now rest in the tender care of our Father, who receives us all just as we are. It is as though in the midst of the darkness and sorrow of the broken planet, a light is shining, and in the center of the beam of light piercing the darkness there is a dance in which the one who was dead celebrates as though he has never died. He is joined in the great dance by the entire community of faith and a great cloud of witnesses without number. This holy celebration, in which death and the fear of death have lost their grip, is one of the gentle graces of Christ—his elegance given to us while we weep and dance and sing—to hold us over until we gain entrance to his eternal kingdom.

Because of this elegance, the unattractive paradox of dying to self to discover the remarkable beauty and strength of individual qualities set in the balance of a grace-filled community actually becomes one of the most attractive propositions a man could ever accept. We don't really like or need our own baggage anyway, so the exchange is positively slanted in our direction. This is true for men and women, for families and churches, for individuals and communities. We could introduce you to Karris, our beautiful friend who for more than nine years has given up everything to live among children in Haiti. When someone reminds her of all she has given up, tears fill her eyes, and she says, "But I have found my life." We could take you to New York, where BJ, an imperfect shepherd—a little Wilberforce, if you will— who lives among the poor and the wealthy in Manhattan, has invested over half his life in the idea that God and his sacred ways are practical for everyday living, so much so that whether a man lives a harsh and isolated life on the streets or a lonely and complex life high on Wall Street, their needs are identical. And we would like you to meet Bill, who has no sons of his own but who, because of his wisdom and kindness, has an entire tribe of young men whose lives have been changed forever. Or you could come to our home, share a meal with us, and allow us to confess our sins and our weaknesses. If you knew us over the years, you would admit we are not the people we once were. The proposition on which we have bet our lives is that Jesus can change us and is making of us more of a miracle of grace than anyone, ourselves included, would have ever expected.

If you do come to our home to spend the night, we'll put you up in the guest room, and when you close the door at night, you will see a homemade coffin standing in the corner like a silent soldier flickering in the moonlight.

Well, not yet. My wife says if I actually build it, she'll have to kill me and put me in it. She's not having "that thing" in our house!

TWELVE

THE CHRIST-MAN

ETHAN WAS ELEVEN WHEN I MET him one Sunday morning as he sat in the back of the auditorium slouched in his father's arms. He did not want to be there. Tired as I was, neither did I. We had an immediate connection. But the little things God does are often important things, so I said a prayer for Ethan and told God it would be very cool if Ethan came forward to the place where I would be serving Communion later in the service.

Halfway through the celebration of the Lord's Supper, Ethan popped out from behind some tall person, suddenly standing in front of me. I didn't see him coming. I hesitated for a split second, then leaned over to look into his eyes, and said. "Ethan, this is the royal feast of our Lord Jesus Christ. This is his body broken for you, and this is his blood that takes away all your sins. This is the peace of Christ, for you." He stood there and looked at me, hands at his side. Then his eyes got big, and he practically shouted, "*Wow!*" as he took the bread and the cup. I was exuberant.

Driving home after the service, I replayed the scene in my mind. What a kind thing for Jesus to show up like that. I was exhausted; Ethan was bummed. And Jesus showed up and gave me the opportunity to be a life giver to a young lad who, in that moment, received a spark of life.

At noon, our family and the relatives who live nearby sat down to one of our fine summer lunches Linda loves to serve. It was exquisite. Perfectly grilled flank steak sandwiches with blue cheese, caramelized onions, and roasted peppers on fresh, hot rolls right from the oven—mouthwatering summer delights. What could be better? I was still high from seeing the lights come on in Ethan's eyes.

As people were leaving, someone made a remark that ticked me off, and in a failed and unnecessary effort to protect myself, I made a comment that cut Linda to the heart. She was kind and waited until everyone was gone and then let me have it. I deserved it. In one moment I had gone from being a life giver to being a life taker. My unkindness actually took the joy out of the experience with Ethan and our family lunch, and what had been a celebration became a dreary afternoon and evening.

Linda and I spent a long time on the porch that evening sitting in our rocking chairs, processing what happened and what was behind it. As we did, she forgave me. In just a few hours, I went from life giver to life taker to life receiver. To me, Ethan looked like another one of those setups orchestrated by God!

At the end of the day, had I become more of a Christ-man? Was I a Christ-man while all of this was going on, and just what is this odd combination of God and man? After his resurrection, Jesus said it was necessary for him to leave, but his Father was going to send the Holy Spirit to live within his followers. Enormous spiritual benefit would accrue to them and to the world, he said, once the third member of the Trinity arrived. His Spirit, Jesus said, would transform orphans into sons and daughters from within. My transformation is obviously still in very wet concrete.

MIXTURES OF "DUST AND DEITY"

Despite all a man's imperfections, this miraculous combining of God's Spirit with the spirit of a man creates something new, which by all visible evidence is at once unlike the old thing yet not entirely like God. What is new retains and restores the unique personality and characteristics of the original man but gives him such a new vantage as though his spirit became simultaneously both older (and wiser) and younger.

The presence of God inside the man cuts off, deep in his spirit, the aging results of sin—not entirely, but noticeably. As the aging of sin is a daily and creeping death, so the renewing of the life-giving spirit within operates day after day, present with us here and now.

This life in the Spirit remains thoroughly rooted in the grit of the real world. People die and lose their minds; life is hard at every level imaginable; parents bury their children. And yet the Spirit lives within as a good professor, tender as a mother, wise like a father, comforting as a friend, to guide us into truth that unleashes us from lies we believed before we became Christ-men. Once captives to our selves, to our half-selves, and to our half-truths, because of God's resident Spirit, we now are free. An odd overstatement describes it for us: "For freedom Christ has set us free."[1] This freedom, this internal Christ-presence, is what distinguishes Christ-men from all other men. Ultimately, only Christ-men have the full capacity to enjoy the completion of their manhood, to develop into who God says a man can be, unique among all of God's creatures.

Freedom, sadly, scares the living daylights out of certain Christ-followers. One day soon, we should apologize for all the ways our fears have made it impossible for others to get acquainted with God. Perhaps those who insist on living as legalists—that is, who return to their old slaveries instead of living in friendship with God and their brothers—can serve once more as our best bad example. These are God's stunted kids. As believers who seek to live by law instead of grace, they must worry about the all-seeing, all-knowing presence of the Holy Spirit within them. What's more, they are still bound to the rules of religious "fruit inspectors." Their worries reveal them to be self-righteous instead of God-righteous. For them, because guilt and shame are still the ugly twins that rule their relationship with God, having a God within who knows everything is the worst kind of bad news imaginable. So when they mess up, they make promises to God that they will never do it again, but before long they do, and they cannot seem to help themselves. In truth, they cannot, because self-help is not the cure.

Legalists must also try to live their lives being good enough for God, afraid he will find them out. But he has already found us out. Every one of us. We are those captives Christ came to set free. He makes it possible to be free from the dominating forces of evil, free from the twisted addiction to ourselves and our bizarre sense of self-importance. For the record, there is almost nothing more impossible to live with than a religious man addicted to himself. But once we are free, we welcome his light. We welcome young ones like Ethan, sent to receive a blessing and to show us something about ourselves, sent to answer general prayers God interprets to have been specific. We appreciate the honesty of our wives, whose voices blend with the Spirit of God within us to help us become Christ-men. We accept "faithful wounds" from a friend when they are intended to bring healing, and we extend mercy and instruction to those who have not yet been made gentle by the Spirit of Christ.

Imagine what might happen if both you and your wife have the same best friend — God — and quit hoping you won't disappoint each other because you know and accept that you will, and because you know your best friend will be there to help you sort out the mess.

If it is entirely true — and it is — that God, who now lives within me, knows all my thoughts and loves me anyway, I have to say two things: God suddenly has become my best friend, and perhaps he was all along the way. I can fear his friendship, which I will do if I do not believe he is good, or I can welcome him and start living an unbelievable life with a new partner and friend. He knows all my sorrows and everything else within me. His Spirit is the searchlight that knows and sees all. And his Spirit makes of my life a light that illuminates dark places so others can find their way. So imagine what might happen if both you and your wife have the same best friend — God — and quit hoping you won't disappoint each other because you know and accept that you will, and because you know your best friend will be there to help you sort out the mess. Your life would be different, and perhaps you, too, would have a hard time remembering why you thought you needed religion when you have a perpetual invitation to enjoy a relationship with God. Behind all intelligence, all experience, all spirituality, then, is the question of what we are and who we are. Modern anthropology deals with the little *who* of our existence—what can be seen through our behavior, our accomplishments, and evolving social patterns—and concludes we are more intelligent than the other animals. Brilliant, but this is the glass ceiling of human reasoning. We see there is more but cannot comprehend it. God invites us to a different view, permitting us to understand the potential he has created in us, a sacred potential most fully expressed in the Christ-man combination. He sees design and personality, not only behavior, identity more than performance, and destiny instead of evolutionary migration. Even more, he lends to us his character and permits us to experience his glory, the transcendent beauty that is the source of our longing and joy. His glory, I hope you are discovering, is present in friendships where he is welcomed.

GREAT IS THE MYSTERY

The question of who God is and who we are in this lively Christ-man combination is compelling and mysterious, a union of the infinite and the finite. This is adequate mystery for both the anthropologist and the theologian. Our old reference point has just been obliterated. Life comes to what was dying, and a new spiritual intelligence has just become possible. This spiritual renovation introduces to the thoughtful anthropologist evidence of possibility and power that surpasses evolutionary progression and produces radical transformation of individuals and entire societies. This is the power of God to reverse the disintegration of all things by interposing spiritual life into the cycles of death and decay. I have become a man in two worlds, joyfully schizophrenic, wonderfully sane, dying but more alive than ever.

Christ and man are an inseparable eternal duo. One is the redeemer who by the power of the resurrection calls men by their new names; the other represents God among his fellows, speaking and doing as best he can what his brother — Christ — tells him to speak and do. This is the beloved culmination of who Christ is, who we are, and who Christ and man are together.

Think of how an artist relates to his canvas or a sculptor to the rock under his chisel. They are infinite by comparison to the lifeless objects under their tools, yet they give life to a flat plane or a common rock. If they have the time, the results are limitless.

I have this theory about God that goes something like this: God creates people because he loves to create and, like every decent artist, to express himself through his art, through his creation. Because God is infinite, he needs billions of us through which to fully express himself. It is why each of us is completely different, yet we bear marks of similarity that are our connection points to each other and to God. What was dust, flat canvas, common rock, is now living, breathing soul, yet God the Artist can do one better. He actually can give his Spirit to live and thrive within his art so it becomes, from every vantage point, inside and out, a multidimensional mystery. He creates in such a unique way that his art can choose whether to accept the Spirit of the Artist or not. This means the art has been invested with intrinsic power to become not less than the original creation but more; to have not less personality but more; to become not less creative but more; and to enjoy a dynamic connection between the living art and the living God. Having Godlike characteristics then, while being fully human, becomes both plausible and true. Yet if he does not receive the Spirit of the Artist, the force of moral, spiritual, and intellectual disintegration becomes inevitable.

A common objection among men who choose to refuse the Spirit of the Artist through the experience of the new birth Jesus offers is that they do not want to lose who they are — their unique personality or way of life. Or they do not, for good reasons, want to become another religious nut job. Rather than try to convince them or merely tell them what they are missing, my proposal for Christ-men is that they become so authentically alive in the Spirit of Christ that others find the offer of the Artist irresistible. To do this, we're going to have to let the Artist pour his life into us and give him space and time to actually complete his beautiful art.

Several years ago, the sweetest friend we ever had died of cancer. That Peggy was the first of our closest friends to die seems both absurd and right. Absurd because, of all people, she deserved to live; right because she was more completed, more finished, than most people we knew.

A few months before she passed, the four couples who walked life together for over twenty-five years met for one last Valentine's dinner. The meal was gourmet fine dining, the benefit of a cooking class the ladies attended, but I doubt any of us remember the menu. What we do remember was what happened during the meal. Peggy never liked to be the center of attention, so before dinner I asked her permission to focus our conversation around our love for her and what her soon departure, short of a miracle, would mean for all of us. She looked into my eyes and said, "I trust you. Do what you think is best."

The idea that we were soon to lose Peggy and yet, as her closest friends, had not talked together with her about this was driving me crazy and had become awkward for all of us. How could we even claim to be friends if did not talk with each other about the hardest thing we ever faced? What would we say later? How is love stronger than death when the memories of a lifetime are mixed with anguish and certain death? Why could we not love Peggy and each other with open emotions, hard as it might be?

To each of us, she is the purest friend we have ever known. The purity in Peggy made friendship with her unique. That Valentine's night, we told Peggy and each other what this friendship, this love, these relationships, and all the struggles of life together had forged in our hearts. The Artist was mixing new colors for us. Later, the nearest words we could find to describe the evening was that we had experienced the glory of God in friendship and the filling of our hearts with joy as sorrow and love flowed down our faces into the sea of God's goodness. God came down to sit with us in the valley of the shadow of death. The ladies poured out their hearts to Peggy, one by one. The beauty of their love for each other was and is profound, and we sat and listened to unusual and eloquent affection poured out like sacred water from the springs of Bethlehem.

What the women said to Peggy would have been enough, but incomplete. The words each of the men added were like the perfect harmony of a beautiful melody. One less talkative brother was eloquent, a gentle power intermingling with his tears and evident in his words. We were quieted by love, and when words could no longer say what we knew and felt within, we broke bread and blessed it, poured wine and prayed, and received from the Lord what he gives when his people share the fellowship of suffering. Spirit and truth made us more present with each other than at any other point in a lifetime of friendship. "Go, sweet love," we said, "but only if you must." Four months later, it was almost impossible to fight our way through tears to carry her coffin to the grave, another tender work of art now complete.

THE ULTIMATE ATTRACTION

So through sorrow and death, as in celebration and joy, the man who is in Christ is learning to live and is being renewed in life day by day. Death strips away the awful pretense. Our conversation about the attraction men feel toward beauty and a man's desire to be on the winning side, even as a spectator at the stadium, now migrates to a deeper and higher place. God's glory is the ultimate attraction of manhood, but because his glory is often invisible, we are lured to exchange the glory of God for things of fractional and temporary beauty. If I take the bait, I am reintroduced to the emptiness I have worked so hard to eliminate from my life. If the glory of God and our relationship with him are indeed the source of joy for the Christ-man, why do we see so few joyful men? When I say joyful, I do not mean merely naive, effeminate, or optimistic. I mean truly joyful and happy men. I think it is precisely because we and our leaders are skilled traders who exchange the glory of God for indulgences that have nearly erased our manhood, and because, in our life together as men, friendship is a shadow of something that exists elsewhere.

But the Christ-man sees the dilemma. Not only has he received a cure for his addiction to himself; he is on a journey with God in which our Father is "bringing many sons to glory" and in which his weaknesses become transparent.[2] God as our friend changes everything. Because God is doing this amazing work in us, Jesus is not ashamed to call us brothers.[3] This band of his brothers, among whom spiritual friendship unlocks the mysteries of men, has what it takes to bring healing and life to everyone around them. We do this with authenticity, honesty, and wisdom, hav-

> **God's glory is the ultimate attraction of manhood, but because his glory is often invisible, we are lured to exchange the glory of God for things of fractional and temporary beauty.**

ing abandoned the false "responsibility" to "fix others," choosing instead to invite our friends and family to become a sanctuary inhabited by Christ's presence.

Inhabited by the glory of God — that is, by the spirit and truth of our Brother — the Christ-man walks the ragged edge between faith and culture. In fact, he does so in such a way that the two become integrated. He learns the dialects of the culture and society in which he lives. He destroys the culture war and replaces it with thoughtful action and life-giving conversation that take thoughts captive to the wisdom of God. He does this because he has joined Christ in the quest of freedom for all men, a quest in which freedom and obedience are no longer antithetical, but magnetic poles that balance our existence. Still capable of evil, we choose what is good.

Out of the blue one day, my son said, "Dad, thanks for not being a zombie." He knows enough of himself and others to know that men are capable of being zombies, of hiding inside shells encasing their dead and dying remains.

"What do you mean?" I replied.

"Most men your age have checked out," he said, "and it is impossible to have a conversation with any of them."

This is the sad truth, but hopefully not the final truth of this generation of men. It's not too late, but none of what you have read here is going to change your life if all you do is tough it out on your own and return to your silent and lonely life. So we're down to a few remaining thoughts and a practical thing or two you might consider for yourself if you want to pour some life back into a worn-out zombie. Accept that you are not perfect and not self-perfectible (to rephrase Peggy Noonan), and neither are your brothers and those you love. Relax. Observe the man who lives. He is a man with friends and a way of life built around intentional friendships. The man with close friends is a man who practices being present in spirit and in truth with those around him. Bitterness repels friends, but a clean and gentle heart welcomes those who otherwise remain strangers but are now close. The Christ-man seeks to welcome all, even the man with the capacity to betray him. He is a man without secrets, through whom light and love pass freely, his humanity complete. As my father liked to say near the end of his life, "My worrying days are past." He had discovered the deep and ancient poetry in the heart of our Father that gives a man his song.

Let it be said of the men in the house: We did not need a movement after all, but just a friend. Let it be said that we offered kindness and friendship to all, when we were men.

There is much more to be said of character, nobility, honor, beauty, truth, and love, but you can say it by your life and by the words in your heart that will resonate in the hearts of your sons and daughters, your spouse, your fellow travelers, and friends as you take courage to speak what you have felt and left unsaid for so long.

Let it be said of the men in the house: We did not need a movement after all, but just a friend. Let it be said that we offered kindness and friendship to all, when we were men.

A PRAYER
FOR EMPTY MEN

Lord, fill my emptiness with your presence,
Replace my desires and my will with your holy passion, with your
  will,
And let the words of my mouth and the meditation of my heart
Be acceptable in your sight, O LORD, my Rock and my Redeemer.

NOTES

CHAPTER 1: LET'S TALK ABOUT MANHOOD

Page 16: *"I will not let you go"*: Genesis 32:26.

Page 20: *"As he thinks"*: Proverbs 23:7 NKJV; *"out of the abundance"*: Matthew 12:34; *"whoever isolates himself"*: Proverbs 18:1.

Page 25: *"when I am weak"*: 2 Corinthians 12:10.

Page 29: *"I will not leave you as orphans"*: John 14:18.

CHAPTER 2: THE WEATHER IS FINE, BUT I'M A LITTLE MESSED UP

Page 32: *"My vitality was drained away"*: Psalm 32:4 NASB.

Page 35: *"Keep your heart with all vigilance"*: Proverbs 4:23.

Page 39: *"Deceit is in the heart"*: Proverbs 12:20.

Page 42: *"Father, forgive them"*: Luke 23:34.

Page 44: who take the kingdom of God by force: Matthew 11:12.

CHAPTER 3: GAME AND STORY — ENTERING THE KINGDOM OF GOD

Page 52: *"He who is noble plans noble things"*: Isaiah 32:8.

Page 59: *"Deliver my soul"*: Psalm 17:13 – 14.

Page 61: *"Your gentleness made me great"*: Psalm 18:35.

Page 62: *"the kingdom of heaven has suffered violence"*: Matthew 11:12.

Page 63: *"Give us this day our daily bread"*: Matthew 6:11.

CHAPTER 4: THE GLORY AND SHAME OF FATHERS AND SONS

Page 68: *"you do not have many fathers"*: 1 Corinthians 4:15.

Page 71: *"The LORD reproves"*: Proverbs 3:12.

Page 72: *"The glory of young men is their strength"*: Proverbs 20:29.

Page 72: *The strength of Jesus is made perfect in our weakness*: 2 Corinthians 12:9.

Page 74: *if there were any who understood*: Psalm 53:2.

Page 74: *he would visit the sins of the fathers*: Exodus 34:7.

Page 75: *"repays to their face those who hate him"*: Deuteronomy 7:10.

Page 75: *"has not believed in the name of the only Son of God"*: John 3:18.

Page 75: *"Know therefore that the LORD your God is God"*: Deuteronomy 7:9.

Page 75: *"sin deceives"*: Genesis 3:13; Romans 7:11; *"sin is crouching at the door"*: Genesis 4:7; *"be sure your sin will find you out"*: Numbers 32:23.

CHAPTER 5: OUR NEED FOR HELP

Page 87: *"Confess your sins to one another"*: James 5:16.

Page 89: *"All men are liars"*: Psalm 116:11 NIV.

Page 92: *"be still, and know"*: Psalm 46:10; *"let not your hearts"*: John 14:1.

Page 93: *"the righteous shall live by faith"*: Romans 1:17.

Page 93: *"faith comes from hearing"*: Romans 10:17.

CHAPTER 7: WHERE THE BEAUTY STARTS

Page 114: *"see through a glass, darkly"*: 1 Corinthians 13:12 KJV.

Page 114: *we beheld his glory*: John 1:14 KJV.

Page 114: *"One thing have I asked of the Lord"*: Psalm 27:4, emphasis mine.

Page 115: *"oaks of righteousness"*: Isaiah 61:3.

Page 116: *wants to awaken sleeping men*: Ephesians 5:14.

Page 118: *"Behold, I stand at the door and knock"*: Revelation 3:20.

CHAPTER 8: SORROW—THE HAND THAT SHAPES US

Page 124: *"all things"* that *"work together for good"*: Romans 8:28.

Page 126: *"it is better to go to the house of mourning"*: Ecclesiastes 7:2.

Page 128: *"a man of sorrows, and acquainted with grief"*: Isaiah 53:3.

Page 128: *"your will be done"*: Matthew 6:10.

Page 130: *the way, the truth, and the life*: John 14:6.

Page 131: *his joy may be in us and that our joy may be full*: John 15:11.

CHAPTER 9: THE TOUGH YEARS

Page 135: *dangerous men who infiltrate*: Jude 11–12.

Page 140: *"he will purify the sons of Levi"*: Malachi 3:2–3.

Page 144: *"Satan has asked to sift you"*: Luke 22:31–32 NIV.

Page 146: *"So also my heavenly Father will do to every one of you"*: Matthew 18:35.

Page 149: *"Father, forgive them"*: Luke 23:34.

CHAPTER 10: SADNESS IN THE CHURCH

Page 151: *a thousand years "are but as yesterday"*: Psalm 90:4.

Page 154: *"occupy"* until his return: Luke 19:13.

Page 159: *"be perfect, as your heavenly Father is perfect"*: Matthew 5:48 KJV.

Page 160: *"My grace is sufficient for you"*: 2 Corinthians 12:9.

Page 161: *"not drink again of the fruit of this vine"*: Matthew 26:29.

Page 162: *love, joy, peace, patience*: Galatians 5:22–23.

CHAPTER 11: BUILD YOUR OWN COFFIN

Page 168: *"May your hearts live forever!"*: Psalm 22:26.

Page 171: *"Let another praise you"*: Proverbs 27:2; *not to think of ourselves more highly*: Romans 12:3.

CHAPTER 12: THE CHRIST-MAN

Page 175: *"For freedom Christ has set us free"*: Galatians 5:1.

Page 176: *"faithful wounds"*: Proverbs 27:6.

Page 181: *"bringing many sons to glory"*: Hebrews 2:10.

Page 181: *not ashamed to call us brothers*: Hebrews 2:11.

ABOUT WES YODER

RAISED ON A DAIRY FARM IN the Amish and Mennonite community of Lancaster, Pennsylvania, Wes Yoder moved to Nashville in 1973 to work in the music business, where he launched the careers of many well-known artists. His projects have included media representation of *The Purpose Driven Life* and literary and media representation of the #1 *New York Times* bestsellers *Mistaken Identity* and *The Shack*. He has appeared on *NBC Nightly News, ABC's Prime Time, Dateline NBC, CNN Headline News,* and others. Wes and his wife, Linda, live in Franklin, Tennessee, and have two children and two grandchildren.

To contact the author or to inquire about speaking engagements, write to Wes@AmbassadorAgency.com. Also be sure to check out www.BondofBrothers.net for more information and to participate in the conversation.

Share Your Thoughts

With the Author: Your comments will be forwarded to the author when you send them to *zauthor@zondervan.com*.

With Zondervan: Submit your review of this book by writing to *zreview@zondervan.com*.

Free Online Resources at
www.zondervan.com

Zondervan AuthorTracker: Be notified whenever your favorite authors publish new books, go on tour, or post an update about what's happening in their lives at www.zondervan.com/authortracker.

Daily Bible Verses and Devotions: Enrich your life with daily Bible verses or devotions that help you start every morning focused on God. Visit www.zondervan.com/newsletters.

Free Email Publications: Sign up for newsletters on Christian living, academic resources, church ministry, fiction, children's resources, and more. Visit www.zondervan.com/newsletters.

Zondervan Bible Search: Find and compare Bible passages in a variety of translations at www.zondervanbiblesearch.com.

Other Benefits: Register yourself to receive online benefits like coupons and special offers, or to participate in research.

ZONDERVAN®

ZONDERVAN.com/
AUTHOR**TRACKER**
follow your favorite authors